MASTERING *the art*
OF MARRIAGE

STAYING TOGETHER WHEN THE WORLD PULLS YOU APART

V. REV. CONSTANTINE NASR

CONCILIAR
PRESS

Chesterton, Indiana

Mastering the Art of Marriage
Staying Together When the World Pulls You Apart

Scripture quotations are taken from the New King James Version,
© 1979, 1980, 1982 by Thomas Nelson, Inc. Used by permission.

Published by   Conciliar Press
                    A division of Conciliar Media Ministries
                    P.O. Box 748
                    Chesterton, IN 46304

Printed in the United States of America

ISBN 10: 1-936270-14-5
ISBN 13: 978-1-936270-14-9

This book is for my wife, Sharon,
without whom there would be no book.
You have been "bone of my bone and flesh of my flesh."
You are my companion, my lover, and my friend.
You are the queen of our home and queen of my heart.

This book is also dedicated to the memory of my parents,
Very Reverend Zacharia and Khouria Nasra Nasr.
Married and with children, they came from Palestine
and made a new life for us in the United States.
In their love for each other, I saw lived out in our home
what it means to master the art of marriage.
May their memory be eternal.

CONTENTS

Acknowledgements

Books are helpful in understanding what it takes to have a successful marriage. But one does not master the art of marriage by simply reading a book and passing an exam on what it said. Successful marriages are the result of wisdom applied to experience. *Mastering the Art of Marriage* is neither an academic treatise on marriage nor a how-to book of easy recipes or easy-to-swallow advice. *Mastering the Art of Marriage* is the culmination of wisdom gained from thirty-eight years of marriage and thirty-seven years of pastoral ministry with couples.

I am indebted to a great number of people for the wisdom shared within these pages. First and foremost, I am indebted to my wife, Sharon. Lessons we have learned in the living of our marriage are scattered throughout the pages of this book.

But a lifetime is too short to figure out marriage on our own. I have learned from the experience of others and the wisdom they have gained. My parents, V. Rev. Zachariah and Kh. Nasra Nasr, and my wife's parents, Charles and Anna Slemon, were a living book of wisdom acquired through the years of their marriages. We learned from them that a successful marriage is not only desirable, it is achievable. But we also learned from watching them that a successful marriage is achieved through working at it.

My thirty-seven years of pastoral ministry have been filled with working with married couples, most of them happy in successful marriages. Collectively, they reinforced the conviction that successful marriages are possible.

As I watched how these couples related to each other, and as I counseled with them through various stages of their lives, I noticed the different techniques they used in mastering the art of being married. Their marriages were not identical, but each had found their own way. They opened my eyes to the multiple possibilities and methods available in creating a successful marriage. I also noticed they did have one thing in common—they were committed to the success of their marriages, and therefore, every one of them was hard at work making that success happen. I am indebted to every one of these couples.

During these same thirty-seven years, I performed countless marriage ceremonies. I saw the excitement and expectancy of having "the perfect wedding" wear off. Within a couple of years, that young couple beaming as they headed off to their reception would be sitting in my office barely speaking to each other.

Often we learn more from failure than success. I noticed patterns in failed relationships. Many couples had married the wrong person and found they were not ultimately compatible. Others entered marriage with stars in their eyes, expecting a happily-ever-after marriage. When disagreements came and the going got tough, they were unwilling to pay the price of hard work to make it through. Lacking a commitment to their marriage, they gave up. Then there were those who never guarded themselves or their marriages. They took their spouses for granted, or they took their marriages for granted, or both. Some cheated with other women or men. Some cheated by making work, or drugs or gambling, more important than their marriages.

From each of them I sadly learned that it is easier to build a good marriage than it is to fix a bad one. I am indebted to each of them for asking me to be part of the crises in their marriages. I bring the lessons learned from these failures to this book.

Finally, I owe a debt of gratitude to Deacon Ezra Ham. Not only did he type the manuscript, but he understood what I wanted to say. It was as if he got inside my head and expressed with an American accent and with contemporary metaphors everything my heart wanted to say. With his collaboration, tentative ideas became fully fleshed-out themes. We worked as with one heart and one mind. We were on the same page, in step with each other. I planted the ideas; he watered the crop. *Mastering the Art of Marriage* is the result. Thank you, my friend.

I want to acknowledge in a special way the assistance given by Archpriest Fr. Peter Gillquist and Katherine Hyde of Conciliar Press. Their suggestions, comments, and editorial expertise have improved my efforts and have made this a better book than it otherwise might have been.

PART I

MASTERING
the art
OF MARRIAGE

IT'S ALL ABOUT RELATIONSHIP

Throughout the years I have been in the ministry, I have learned from first-hand experience that a successful marriage requires a commitment—one that includes work, adaptation, and martyrdom of the will. I have also witnessed the dynamic life that is the result of such a commitment. This commitment can produce the miracle of a man and a woman becoming one flesh within a marriage that is beautiful and enriching to both husband and wife.

For Orthodox Christians, marriage is a sacrament; it is holy for those who love Christ and are obedient to His will. "'For this reason a man shall leave his father and mother and be joined to his wife, and the two shall become one flesh.' So then, they are no longer two but one flesh. Therefore what God has joined together, let not man separate" (Matthew 19:5–6).

I married my wife, Sharon, when I was 28 years old. I met her at a parish life conference in Boston in 1972, and was attracted to her by her dress and her eyes. I found a way of meeting her, and our courtship had lasted less than three months before we began to speak of marriage. Somehow, by God's grace, He blessed me with the gift of life with this woman. We "dated" by telephone, and after I had paid two visits to her home in Pawtucket, Rhode Island, we were married.

We did not participate in any marriage encounters, nor did we attend any marriage enrichment classes. My understanding of marriage and my education in how to be a husband came from observing how my parents lived and acted, how they related to each other when facing serious issues and challenges, how they exercised patience with each other, and how they resolved issues. I also learned from Sharon's parents. They were a wonderful model of what a loving marriage looks like when two people become one flesh. The words of Proverbs held true for us: "Train up a child in the way he should go, and when he is old he will not depart from it" (Proverbs 22:6).

This is not to suggest our parents never faced difficult times. There were times when tempers grew short and they shouted in frustration. At times tears were shed. And I would be lying if I said I did not have difficulties and serious challenges in my life with my wife. But a marriage grows when two people discover common ground and how to stand side by side in facing the challenges. We faced all our crises with respect and sensitivity to each other. Most importantly, we never took our marriage or each other for granted.

For thirty-eight years, Sharon and I have been working on our marriage. We talk about our marriage and our life together. We seek wisdom and counsel from other couples with successful marriages. We read on the subject. We also have learned from the mistakes of others whose marriages did not survive. In short, we are always working on our relationship.

When I was ordained a priest in 1973, I was newly married myself, and I needed guidance in counseling young couples for the sacred and holy union of marriage. I was eager to learn for the sake of those I was counseling, and being a newlywed, for my own sake as well.

After thirty-eight years of reading, studying, and offering marriage counseling, after countless hours dealing with marriages in conflict, I am convinced that I need to share with you what I have learned about marriage. There are dangers to be avoided. But there are also insights to be learned and wisdom to be gained.

A scene in the movie *Four Christmases* shows couples in a dance class learning how to dance at their weddings. When asked when the date of their wedding will be, the characters played by Vince Vaughn and Reese Witherspoon pour out an anti-marriage spiel about how they come from divorced homes and why would they want to ruin their relationship with something they had to work at called marriage. Of course, by the end of the movie they discover the meaning and value of families.

Couples eagerly take dance lessons before their wedding because they don't want to embarrass themselves at the wedding reception. Vaughn and Witherspoon's characters were willing to put out the effort to learn how to dance together, but they were unwilling to put out the effort to make a marriage work.

A successful marriage does not happen nonchalantly. Like an intricate dance, marriage is the art of two people learning how to move gracefully through life in step with each other. To become an accomplished dancer requires many lessons over several years. Learning how to move gracefully through life in step with your spouse will require weekly if not daily effort. It is never too late to learn how to dance. Nor is it too late to master the art of marriage. It will take a lifetime of lessons, but that's what marriage is: a lifetime of moving gracefully through life in step together.

Throughout the years I have collected much information on marriage that has improved my skills both as a counselor and as a husband. From this information I have created practical exercises that couples just like you have found very useful in learning how to talk with each other about themselves and their hopes and dreams for their marriage.[1]

No one wants their marriage to fail. That's why you're reading this book. Whether you're in the courtship stage or married, whether this is your first marriage or a second, whether you've hit a rocky spot in your marriage or you're doing preventive maintenance by looking for ways to improve your marriage, this book is for you.

Remember when you first fell in love? Remember how you gushed over her, bought her flowers, and took her on dates? Remember how you wanted to share every moment with him and thought he was the best man on earth?

Most of us have been there. So we decide to get hitched, settle down, and tie the knot—we decide to get married. We make grand plans for what the wedding day will be like. What will we wear? What will we say? Where will we go?

We spend months and months planning for that one big day, but what about the days, weeks, months, and years to follow? How much time do we spend planning what that will look like? Unfortunately, we get so caught up in planning for the wedding that we overlook preparing for the marriage.

And because we did not prepare for the marriage:

- ✎ Now you'd rather go out with the guys than with your girl.
- ✎ The only flowers you buy are for a day of yard work.

---

1 I have tried to cite every source. But some information has become so much a part of me that I no longer remember what its source might be.

- ✍ The only dates in your life are shriveled-up fruits.
- ✍ If you have to spend another minute together, it might be your last.
- ✍ You wonder if you'd want him if he were the last man on earth.[2]

Television has given us *Desperate Housewives*. But we are also a nation of desperate husbands and desperate marriages. When we look at the basic institutions that undergird society, such as the family, religion, politics, and education, the majority of them are in various degrees of collapse around us.

One thing that is not collapsing is the Orthodox Church. The Church plays an important role in the life of the home and family. It represents an oasis of sanity in the midst of a nation that has lost its consensus on values. Knowing that over half of our marriages end in divorce, one can easily be discouraged and, just as Vince Vaughn and Reese Witherspoon's characters did, pour out an anti-marriage spiel.

This book is written to offer hope. A successful marriage is possible, but it won't happen by accident. It has been said that marriages may be made in heaven, but they are lived on earth. It is on earth that the work of mastering the art of marriage takes place.

The primary focus of this book is on the internal realities of a marriage. We do not marry our spouse's father or mother, tribe or friends. We marry a beloved partner who needs all the care and attention we can give, not just for the weeks or days leading to the wedding, but for the days, months, and years to follow. Marriage partners commit themselves to each other, in the words of Protestant ceremonies, "for better, for worse, for richer, for poorer, in sickness and in health, forsaking all others, so long as we both shall live."

In real estate, the three most important qualities of a successful property are said to be "location, location, location." The three most important qualities of a successful marriage are "relationship, relationship, relationship." This book focuses on the two of you and how you can become one.

---

2 Brian Bolton, *Desperate Marriages*. Downloaded from SermonCentral.com on 12/21/2005.

AND THE TWO SHALL BE ONE

Television shows such as *The Bachelor* and *The Bachelorette* have trivialized relationships into little more than the product of window shopping in a variety of exotic locales. Online dating services are modern-day matchmakers where marriages are arranged by computers instead of parents. Having "made a connection," people who use these services believe they have "found their soul mate." With their "compatibility" assured by a computer, after a few dates, they start planning a wedding. Often writing their own vows, couples pledge their forever-love to each other and get married.

But sooner or later—sometimes sooner—the honeymoon is over. During the courtship, both seek to sell themselves to the other by putting their best foot forward, showing kindness and courtesy. But as they settle into the daily routine of life, kindnesses and courtesies, which should increase and strengthen their affection and love, instead begin to diminish.

How many wives have found themselves thinking, after a few years of marriage:

- He used to open the door for me.
- He used to wait for me.
- He used to bring me flowers or candy.
- He used to remember my birthday.
- We used to go on dates.
- We used to linger over long lunches.
- He used to spend time with my family.
- He used to spend money on me.

- ∽ He used to be sensitive to my needs.
- ∽ He used to really listen and hear me.
- ∽ He used to share his thoughts with me.

And of course the husband has his own corresponding list:

- ∽ She used to encourage me to play golf.
- ∽ She used to wear sexy nighties.
- ∽ She used to prepare my favorite meals.
- ∽ She used to come meet me for lunch.
- ∽ She used to buy me special aftershave.
- ∽ She used to hold hands in the car.
- ∽ She used to want a fire in the fireplace.
- ∽ She never used to have those darned headaches.

When the "used-tos" take over—when the past looks better than the present—your relationship is in trouble. We so easily work at selling ourselves to begin a relationship, but just as easily fail to work at growing our relationship and mastering the art of marriage. Left unattended, the "used-tos" lead to a declining spirit, and the marriage ultimately ends in divorce.

Connections may be instantaneous, but relationships are not. Relationships are developmental. Two people, male and female, who may be complete opposites, are called to become one. This is not a one-time act or a single event. Relationships have to grow, deepen, and mature.

The account of the creation of man and woman found in Genesis 2 gives us insights into the developmental nature of relationships. In verse 18, God, who has created a man and placed him in a garden in Eden to cultivate it, says, "*It is* not good that man should be alone; I will make him a helper comparable to him."

Relationships keep us from being alone. But not being alone is more than simply not being by ourselves. You can be on a crowded bus and still feel all alone. Being alone means not having anyone else with whom to share our inner thoughts and feelings. Two people can be married and still be all alone if their dating relationship does not become a marriage relationship in which they increasingly become more open towards each other in sharing their deepest thoughts and feelings. It is not good to be alone. And if one is married and still alone inside the marriage, not only is it not good, it can prove disastrous.

"I will make him a helper comparable to him." Our spouses are not hired hands. Nor are they our servants. They are helpers comparable to us. They are our companions, and together we form a mutually beneficial relationship in which we aid, support, and encourage each other as very best friends and lovers. In much the same way that God is "a very present help in trouble" (Psalm 46:1), we are to be a help to our spouses.

In our modern society, men and women are running away from the responsibility of being helpers suitably paired in a relationship that gives aid and care for their mutual benefit. They instead look for the first opportunity to take the easy way out. We must know up front that it is the role of the husband and wife to labor as one in preserving and protecting their relationship. Their relationship is best protected when they allow themselves to grow in learning how to take care of each other and how to be a help to each other. This will require time and involves much trial and error, and great patience with each other.

There are no perfect marriages. One can watch the soap operas on television and think that is what a marriage is. Our movies, like our fairy tales, are about falling in love and living happily ever after. But a marriage is not a fairy tale; it is reality. Marriage is not a fantasy lived out in dreamland. Marriages are filled with crises, sweat, and tears as well as with romance and laughter.

As we begin looking into the personalities of a couple, we will find that each couple is unique, with its own special identity; we will also find that each person making up the couple is unique, with his or her own special identity. But there is a common thread that draws the two together and gives them a common ground of compatibility. Your relationship is not magical but is created out of real likes and dislikes, real strengths and weaknesses.

As you as a couple do the various worksheets in the pages ahead, your personal awareness will build as each of you evaluates and takes into serious consideration the physical, emotional, intellectual, and spiritual dimensions within yourself and your spouse.

Today in the United States, slightly over half of our marriages end in divorce. Sadly, the disintegration of marriages is directly linked to declines in the church and in educational and governmental institutions that used to offer direction and encourage the healing of two people and their relationship. Today sixty percent, if not more, of our society comes from broken homes. The splintering of the church into thousands of denominations is now mirrored in multiple thousands of splintered marriages. A loss of moral values in our educational system, coupled with governmental compromises on family values, now makes getting a divorce acceptable social and public policy. In some states, for twenty-five dollars you can now file for a divorce.

The model of parents, grandparents, and great-grandparents who stayed together is almost gone. We live in a transient and mobile society. We have lost our roots and no longer build on the foundation of family values or family history. We have severed our connection with the past, in the persons of our parents and grandparents, and many refuse to embrace the future by choosing not to have children and grandchildren. With no past and no future, we live only in the present. Life becomes all about "me" and my pleasure in this moment.

A good friend, also an Orthodox priest, was speaking to a group of fifty or sixty college men on the subject of marriage. It was a Christian talk in a secular setting.

In the question-and-answer session that followed, one young man raised his hand to be recognized. "I'm in love with the greatest girl on earth," he said. "She's everything I've ever hoped for. But I'm scared to death."

"Why is that?" my friend asked.

"I'm not sure we can stay married. In my family, my grandfather cheated on my grandmother, and they're divorced. My dad cheated on my mom, and they're divorced."

And with tears running down his cheeks in the presence of his buddies, he sobbed, "Is there any hope for me?"

"This is what conversion to Christ is," my friend answered. "When we give our lives to Him, it's a new beginning, a fresh start. If the two of you allow Jesus Christ to be head of your home, and live your lives within His Church, you've got a great shot at making it.

"And here's the added opportunity for you," said my friend. "You get to be the guy in your family who breaks this chain of failure! Your sons and daughters will love you for it."

Visit any state website and look for national vital statistics reports on marriage and divorce. It may cause you, like the young man my friend encouraged, to wonder whether your own marriage will be just another divorce statistic.

Not surprisingly, Nevada leads the nation in its divorce rate. But we are shocked to learn that Arkansas is number two. In Oklahoma (where I live) in 1997, there were 28,000 marriages and 22,000 divorces.[3] A general might send 28,000 troops into a battle even if he knew in advance only 6,000 would survive. But they certainly would never be new, untrained recruits.

In the marriage encounters I lead, I request participants to look for the record of marriages and divorces for their own county. I ask that they give me the daily totals and determine the average for the week. Then they determine the ratio of marriages to divorces. Try it for yourself and your county. It will bring home the point that the issue of disintegrating marriages is not a problem that exists somewhere "out there." It is a problem happening in the county in which you live.

The fragmentation of Christianity fosters a climate conducive to the dissolution of the family. Removing prayer from our public schools has increased secular humanism. And the media have also contributed to moral decline. Frank Schaeffer is correct when he declares we are living in a post-Christian era. The Church is the only vehicle that can restore and strengthen the sacrament of marriage. Our prayer for you is that you will protect and guard your marriage relationship.

If your spouse, fiancé, or significant other will do so, read this book together, out loud. Do the suggested exercises together. Relax and have some fun with them. Mull over what these pages make you think about. Quietly discuss your thoughts with each other. Perhaps by the end of the book you will find yourselves talking with each other more. Perhaps you will find that your relationship has grown, your love has deepened, and your commitment to each other has strengthened. And should that be the case, you may find yourselves hearing the Orthodox blessing, "God grant you many years!"

---

3 Fr. John Maxwell, "Marriage in the 90s," in *The Mustard Seed* (Ft. Smith, Arkansas: SS. George & Alexandra Orthodox Christian Mission, June, 1998), 1.

SO, HOW DID THE TWO OF YOU MEET?

It's natural to wonder how two people met. There are many avenues for meeting someone—through family, friends, church events, work, or in social settings. Your relationship is special, and it is worth remembering and writing down how you met.

How did you meet? _____

_____

_____

_____

When did you meet? _____

_____

_____

Where did you meet? _____

_____

_____

What was the special attraction?
- ❏ Their eyes?
- ❏ Their skin color?
- ❏ Their hair?

- ❏ Their voice?
- ❏ Their style of clothes?
- ❏ Their physical beauty?
- ❏ Their elegance?
- ❏ Their intelligence?
- ❏ Their smile?
- ❏ Their spirit?
- ❏ Their family?
- ❏ Their humor?
- ❏ Their career?
- ❏ Their car?
- ❏ Their bank account?

Each one of us is attracted differently. We are visual creatures, especially men, and often the attraction is based on what we see. (Of course, if someone is unable to see, the first impression could come from the voice.) If we feel an attraction, then we are drawn to speak to each other and decide whether we want to invest more time in getting to know each other. The more we get to know someone, if we like the real person "inside the skin," the better-looking he or she becomes.

Relationships progress, develop, and move through stages of walking and talking together and enjoying each other's company. As emotions deepen, we express our growing relationship by holding hands and showing affection.

Each one of us should write down his or her story. It is interesting and valuable for a couple then to compare their stories, to discover the similarities and the differences in how they understand the beginning of their relationship.

There are many reasons people decide to marry. Some marry because they have found a partner in life whom they love. Others get married out of necessity, financial accommodation, or even jealousy: "My sister got married, so now I want to get married." Others marry because they are getting older and want to settle down. Some marry because of family pressure. Others marry because they have fallen in love. But "love" in this sense is a tricky reason. Those who have fallen in love in one breath can fall out of love in the next.

Saying "yes" to marriage is a huge decision. You cannot walk down the aisle with your fingers crossed, thinking, "If it doesn't work out, I can always get a divorce." You must search your own heart and evaluate your commitment to having a partner for life. At the end of the movie *The Wedding Date*, the main character says, "I started to walk away, but I decided I would rather fight with you than make love with someone else." He was saying, "I would rather have you as my partner and work through our disagreements than be with anyone else." It should be difficult to say yes. Remember, it is even more difficult and heartbreaking to say, "I want a divorce."

I have asked you to think about when and how you met each other. I have asked you to write out your story and share it with your partner. I am sharing with you the wisdom I have learned over the last thirty-eight years. I think it's only fair that you know my story as well.

I was not planning to get married. I wanted to remain celibate. But my parents wanted grandchildren. I do love children, so I began to consider marriage. It was at this time I decided to attend a church convention in Boston.

I knew a few friends in the Boston area, and soon the word was out that this seminarian was looking for a bride. At the Saturday evening dance, as I sat with Metropolitan Philip, the primate of the Antiochian Archdiocese, and several priests, a bevy of beautiful young ladies were introduced to me by their pastors. I felt embarrassed and wanted to fly away.

During the dancing, a young lady in a beautiful gown caught my eye. I began to ask about her and found out she was an Orthodox Christian, a member of St. Mary Church in Pawtucket, Rhode Island. The host priest for the convention was her pastor. I pointed her out to him, and he promised to introduce her to me.

During the intermission he went to get her. I got cold feet. All I could think about was being embarrassed all over again, or even being rejected, so I left the room! When I returned, both the metropolitan and the priest were quite upset with me.

Later that evening I did meet her. We took a walk and began a conversation that has now lasted almost four decades. She was a hairstylist. I was a barber at the seminary. We had a common denominator to break the ice in getting to know one another. I visited her in Pawtucket three times. After a few phone calls, we began to speak of marriage, and soon we were engaged.

I was in the last year of my studies at the seminary. We lived four hours apart, so there was no daily or even weekly dating. I was busy with my studies, but on January 7, 1973, Sharon Slemon and I were married at St. Mary Church in Pawtucket, Rhode Island.

I believe God was at work in bringing Sharon and me together. And we are at work to make our marriage last for eternity. To this day her eyes, her style of dress, and her personality still catch my eye and take my breath away.

Each one has his or her own unique story to tell. Now it's Sharon's turn to tell the story of our meeting and courtship from her perspective.

SHARON'S STORY

It was Father's Day Weekend, June 1972. I was 24 years old, which at that time was considered old for a young woman to be still unmarried. I had begun to fear I would never meet my *naseeb*—the Arabic term for the man it was my destiny to marry.

My friends and I were attending the New England Region Church Convention in the Boston area. Since it was such a small region, everyone knew everyone at the convention, but that year we had a new face—a young seminarian from St. Vladimir Seminary. He had come in order to mention to Metropolitan Philip Saliba that he was going overseas to try to meet a young lady in the old country and get married. The metropolitan said to him, "In all of America and Canada you could not find anyone!"

That evening at the dance, all the regional priests were bringing women to the table for Constantine to meet. Finally, he pointed me out in the dance line and said, "That is the one I want to meet." The bishop asked, "Who does this girl belong to?" and my parish priest, Fr. Athanasius Saliba (who is now a bishop in Lebanon), answered, "She belongs to me!" Fr. Athanasius came to my table and took me to the metropolitan. We talked, and he said to me, "I would like you to talk with one of my sons." (He calls his seminarians his "sons.")

In the meantime, Constantine had disappeared. I went back to my friends and told them that if he wanted to talk to me he would have to pay. Each parish always had one girl who would do an Arabic dance to raise money for the church, and I was the one representing my parish. As I danced

I took several one-dollar bills from Constantine, a poor seminarian. When the dancing was over, he introduced himself to me, and we just started visiting with each other. The evening passed, and we never went back to the party. We exchanged names and phone numbers.

The convention concluded, he went back to New York, and I went back to Rhode Island. A few days later, I received a letter from him stating he would like to come visit. I asked my mother, and she said, "You have to invite him; remember, the metropolitan asked you to talk with him." There was no way out—you don't say no to the metropolitan! So, being the obedient daughter I am to my parents and to the Church, I invited Constantine to Rhode Island.

A few weeks passed and he came to Pawtucket, staying at the home of my priest. We went out that weekend; he came back another time, and after the third evening out, he said he wanted to speak to my father. The next evening he visited with my father (my mother and I were there also), explaining what his life would be like and how I would be part of this "clergy world," because it is a unique life that we live. I told my parents this was what I wanted, especially since my whole life up to that point had been family, friends, and church; I wasn't the type that went out casually. I believe my parents had raised me for this position in life—not that I was or am special, but just that this fulfills my being. I love it!

Up to this point Constantine had not mentioned any of this to his family. Now it was time for both sets of parents to find out about each other. My father called Fr. Athanasius and asked about Constantine's parents, and his parents called Fr. Athanasius asking the same questions about my parents. Metropolitan Philip also talked to my priest about me and my family—it was like a government investigation!

Finally, it was agreed we would get engaged in August 1972, and the wedding date was set for January 1973. Believe me, it was a fast six months.

The first six months of our marriage also went fast. We were married in January in Pawtucket; Constantine was ordained deacon in March in Beckley, West Virginia, graduated from St. Vladimir Seminary in May, and was ordained priest in June in Rhode Island. We moved to our first parish, St. George Church in Cedar Rapids, Iowa, in July. It was a whirlwind experience; but, thank God, it has been an adventure I would repeat if I had the opportunity.

God truly takes care of you if you give yourself to Him—His time, His place, His guidance. In these thirty-eight years, Fr. Constantine and I have shared so many different experiences, and God has helped us through every one. I'm not saying it has been a smooth road all the way, but somehow we have always managed to get through whatever has come in front of us.

Whatever your life will bring before you, don't hesitate to ask God for help—He will always respond in His time and way. Keep your faith strong even if times seem unbearable. I remember Fr. Constantine's uncle telling us the night before we got married, "Always be best friends with each other because that's all you have, each other, and never go to bed mad at each other." I have always kept these thoughts in my heart and mind. We have worked hand-in-hand all these years, a team effort—supporting and managing our life as one unit, always focusing on the important things. Keep your heart clear and your faith strong, and you will pass the thirty-eight-year test (and more!) just as we have.

MIRROR, MIRROR ON THE WALL

In the children's story *Snow White*, the queen, admiring her own beauty, often asks her magic mirror who is the fairest one of all. But magic mirrors are no different from real mirrors: they cannot lie. They can only show what is there. Like the queen, we do not like it when the mirror won't lie. We do not like seeing gray hair and wrinkles appear. We do not like to admit that we are not everything we think we are. We especially do not like admitting any negative things about ourselves.

If we do not like admitting negative things about ourselves, we certainly do not like others to see any of our negatives. Like Jim Carrey's character in *The Mask*, we all wear masks. Masks create a public persona by which we want to be known. They also disguise and cover up who we really are.

There are many problems with masks. It takes great effort to keep up the public front in order to be someone we are not. By disguising who we really are, we never allow our true self to grow and mature. In a marriage, masks are absolutely catastrophic.

The Bible tells the story of Jacob, who falls in love with Rachel. At their wedding his father-in-law switches brides, and Jacob unknowingly marries Rachel's older sister, Leah. He does not discover he has been tricked until the morning after they have consummated the marriage. Veils can also serve as masks!

During the dating and courtship period, both parties are putting their best foot forward. While we may not be pretending to be someone we're not, we do try to hide our negative qualities from each other. There is truth in the saying, "Love is blind." Many a groom thought he was marrying a Rachel, only to discover later he had married a Leah. And many a bride thought she was marrying a Jacob, sadly to discover he was an Esau instead.

Some women ignore the negatives they see because they believe, falsely, that once married they will be able to change their husband and correct his negatives. This is yet another recipe for disaster. What you see is what you get. We must, as much as possible, be honest with the one we love. They must know us for who we really are and love us as we are.

	Known to self	Unknown to self
Known to others	My Public Self	My Blind Spots
Unknown to others	My Hidden Self	My Unconscious Self

In the Johari Window,[4] shown above, a person is represented as a window with four panes. One pane is our public self: what we know about ourselves that others know also. The second pane represents our blind spots. This is that part of us that others see, but we don't see about ourselves. The third pane is our hidden self: the private things we know about ourselves but no one else knows. The last pane is that part of us that is unknown both to us and to others: our unconscious self.

For us to grow and mature, our relationship with our partner must also grow. That is really the key storyline in the movie *Four Christmases*. Every couple in the movie seems to know more about each other than do the characters played by Vince Vaughn and Reese Witherspoon. Vaughn and Witherspoon's characters discover unknown things about each other and have to decide whether they want their relationship to grow, even when such growth requires stepping outside the limited boundaries of what they already know.

---

4 The Johari Window is named for its creators, **Jo**seph Luft and **Har**ry Ingram, who created the window in 1955.

The growth of our marriage involves the process of letting our spouse help us see our blind spots. It takes great love and humility to trust our partner in this way.

In this chapter, we will begin looking into the mirror to discover any blind spots we may have, especially regarding our negative tendencies. In the next chapter we will explore our blind spots regarding our positive traits.

You and your partner should each take a piece of paper. At the top of the sheet, write *Blind Spot Negatives*. Create two columns. Label the left column *My Negative Tendencies*. Label the right column _____'s *Negative Tendencies*, using your partner's name.

EXERCISE 1

BLIND SPOT NEGATIVES

My Negative Tendencies   _____'s **Negative Tendencies**

Please remember, this exercise should be done together. First, privately begin listing all the negative tendencies you think you have. Secondly, after you have completed your list, begin thinking of some of the negative tendencies you see in your partner. And thirdly, come together and share your lists.

To begin the sharing process, one of you should share your list of the negatives you see in yourself. Go slowly and tell what you mean and why you think this is true about you. Your partner should check their list to see if they listed the same trait for you. If they did not list a given item, they should comment on the fact that they don't see that trait in you even though you see it in yourself. Proceed all the way through your negative list.

Now it's your partner's turn to share their negative list about themselves. They should follow the same process as before, explaining what they mean and why they think they have each item on their list. You should follow your list to see whether you have their items on your list about them.

One goal is to find those common denominators on which you can build your relationship. On the basis of this exercise and the one in the next chapter, you will see what draws the two of you together. You will discover areas where you are alike. For example, you both may have the same negative or positive trait. You will also discover areas where you agree. For example, you may both agree that one of you is a worrywart.

A second goal is to realize that real differences also exist. You are two separate individuals. You each have your own identity and your own personality. In a healthy marriage we do not lose our identities or personalities.

The Holy Trinity is Three Persons—Father, Son, and Holy Spirit. The Trinity is not an amorphous sameness. The Three Persons of the Trinity, while sharing the one Divine Nature, nevertheless never lose their personal identities. The Father is not the Son, the Son is not the Holy Spirit, nor is the Holy Spirit the Father. In our marriages, the husband is not the wife, and the wife is not the husband. We form a complete whole, but we each bring our unique personality into that whole. Real differences, in and of themselves, are not a threat to a healthy marriage when those differences add to and help strengthen our commitment to a lifelong relationship.

Of course it is possible that fundamental differences may exist that mitigate against long-term compatibility and serve to undermine a commitment to a shared life together. Sometimes these fundamental differences in goals, purposes, and compatibilities are sugar-coated and glossed over by all the positive things shared in common. A failure honestly to acknowledge that fundamental differences do, in fact, exist can lead, once the sugar-coating melts and the glow of the romance fades under the stress of married life, to a failure of the marriage.

In a small-group session of engaged couples, George volunteered that he was an avid, incurable game hunter. Though they had known each other for nearly a year, this was the first his fiancée, Carol, had heard of it. "George, I can't imagine ever killing anything!" she protested.

"But I dress and freeze the meat for my meals, and give some away to others. It's not killing for killing's sake," he responded. "Nothing goes to waste."

"Killing is killing," she insisted.

"But Carol, you order steak when we go out for dinner. Somebody had to . . ."

"Hold it!" said the group leader.

This was an honest disagreement, and one George and Carol decided they could live with. He still hunts, she still orders steak on their evenings out, and they are very happily married.

In a healthy marriage, shared goals and mutual compatibility realistically encompass and include differences, both positive ones and negative ones. The exercises here and in the next chapter are designed to help us identify the common ground that cements us together as well as to discover and confess that differences also exist. When we embrace our partner, we also embrace and accept their negative as well as positive traits.

I have listed below actual negative traits or behaviors that participants in my marriage encounter seminars have listed. Perhaps some of them will appear on your list for yourself or your partner.

NEGATIVE TRAITS OR BEHAVIOR

Proud

Stubborn

Easily frustrated

Quick to be defensive

Short-tempered

Does not ask for help

Lets people take advantage

Denies things they did

Doesn't own up to mistakes

Won't admit shortcomings

Jaded worldview

Paranoid

Pessimistic

Negative about the future

Non-Christian background

Bad childhood

Profuse curser

No self-discipline

Doesn't follow through

Paranoid & suspicious

Spoiled

Socially abrasive

Not fiscally responsible

Poor work ethic

Always spending

Assumes others' problems

Not always fully honest

Doesn't open up and share

Selfish

Overly possessive

Not assertive enough

Worries too much

Thinks too much

Messy housekeeper

A slob

Too much a loner

Too independent

Too timid

Hates to cook

Has poor judgment

Always critical

Criticizes others

Not focused

Inflexible

High anxiety level

Prejudiced

Insensitive to others

Rigid

Closed-minded

Lacks feelings

Ignores me

Procrastinates

Not understanding

Unkind when under pressure

Overly protective

I wish I were closer to God

Sarcastic

Not a good listener

Only does things their way

Braggart

Afraid to share feelings

Overly sensitive

Blabs everything

Self-centered

Overbearing

Likes to argue

Always late

Gullible

Annoying personal habits

Bites their nails

Not a good communicator

Is not a grateful person

Lazy

Not outgoing personality

Doesn't realize own limits

Keeps me from my family

Insecure

Poor self-image

Poor self-esteem

Too negative about self

Neglects health

Poor diet

Poor exercise

Obsessed with exercise

Obsessed with appearance

Not patient

Puts others before me

Easily upset or bothered

Moody

Thinks they're always right

Unforgiving

Doesn't tolerate mistakes

Over-confident

Over-focuses on details

Does things without planning

A doubter

A worrier

Just a messy person

Has non-verbal moods

Manipulative

Crisis seeker

Not completely honest

Seldom prompt

Easily deceived

Perfectionist

Unrealistic high standards

Never offers praise

Never listens

Tied to home

Loves athletics

Lets others walk all over her

Emotionally delicate

Conceited
Does not keep promises
Unjustifiably jealous
Too hard on herself
Too blunt and outspoken
Speaks harshly
Likes to play the victim
Doesn't want children
Not a gracious host
Clumsy
Not graceful
Not gentle
Refuses to move on in life
Poor personal hygiene
Unhealthy habits
Loves chocolates and sweets
Drinks too much
Smokes too much
Bad addictions
Drug addiction
Coarse in speech
Bottles things inside
Can't keep a secret
Can't keep quiet
Can't live within a budget
Arrogant
Prideful

Afraid of intimacy
Shows a lack of emotion
Doesn't care about family
Doesn't like having friends
Talks about past boyfriends
Talks about past girlfriends
Not romantic
Not passionate
Easily intimidated
Won't stand up for himself
Analyzes everything
Dwells on the past
Too materialistic
Too critical
Too inflexible
Too impulsive
Too structured
Too dull
Too serious
Too demanding
Too strict
Never available
Never has time for me
Overschedules life
Forgetful
One-track mind
A know-it-all

That's quite a list of real negatives that have been shared in my seminars. Negatives are real, and we all have them. By gently talking about our negatives with our partner, we minimize their power to be a ticking time bomb waiting to destroy our relationship.

Remember, in the Johari Window we all have blind spots. Our friends see our negatives and accept us anyway. Our partner knows our negatives and loves us anyway. Let our love for each other give us the courage to learn how those who love us most see us.

LITTLE PIGS AND STURDY HOMES

Everyone born in the United States knows the children's story of the Three Little Pigs. Each pig sets out to build his house. The first pig builds his of straw. The second pig builds his house of sticks, while the third pig builds his house out of bricks. Soon the big bad wolf comes upon the first little pig, who runs into his home for safety. The wolf huffs and puffs and blows the straw house down. In order to escape, the first little pig runs to the stick home of the second little pig. The wolf follows him and huffs and puffs until the house of sticks also falls down. The two little pigs run to the third little pig's home. Try as he might, this time the big bad wolf is unable to blow down the sturdy house made of bricks.

More is at work in this story than the relative merits of various building materials. Obviously, bricks are stronger than straw or sticks. The deeper theme of the story is about building our lives. The story cautions us that we should build our lives carefully by deliberately choosing those qualities that will help us survive the storms of life.

There comes the time to leave mom and dad's home and build our own life and our own home. Like the three little pigs, we must decide what kind of stuff we will use to build our lives and our homes. If we and our homes are to survive, we should build our character and our marriages not on fluff, but on brick-solid qualities.

In the last chapter we focused on the blind spots in our lives that can prove destructive to our relationships. In this chapter we will focus on the positive things, the sturdy bricks we can use to build strong relationships, strong marriages, and strong homes.

As we saw previously, the growth of our marriage involves the process of letting our spouse help us see our blind spots. It takes great love and humility to trust our partner in this way. This is just as true for our positive traits as it was for our negative ones.

Sometimes it is easier to focus on negatives than on positives. It is easier to criticize ourselves or our partner than it is to acknowledge the positives in our lives and theirs.

For a relationship to grow, we must be willing to drop our mask enough to be honest and trust our partner with our private heart. Our partner must know how sacred such a moment of vulnerability is. To let our mask slip is to risk being misunderstood, laughed at, or ignored. It is also to risk being loved so much in return that another now guards our private heart with their love.

The turning point in the movie *The Proposal* comes when Sandra Bullock's character, Margaret Tate, and Ryan Reynolds' character, Andrew Paxton, inadvertently bump into each other while going to and from a shower—and both are naked. Immediately following this metaphorical unmasking moment, fully clothed by blankets and darkness, Margaret Tate opens up and begins to share her heart with Andrew.

All relationships have such moments. Marriage involves not only physical nakedness but psychological and sociological nakedness as well. It is simply impossible to hide from our spouse. Eventually he or she will catch us in the act of being ourselves. And eventually we will grow tired of wasting so much energy hiding in our own home from our own spouse.

In our last chapter we looked into the mirror to discover any blind spots we might have regarding our negative tendencies. Now we are ready to explore our blind spots regarding our positive traits.

You and your partner should each take a piece of paper. At the top of each sheet write: *Blind Spot Positives*. Create two columns. Label the left column *My Positive Tendencies*. Label the right column _____ *'s Positive Tendencies*, using your partner's name:

EXERCISE 2

BLIND SPOT POSITIVES

Complete this exercise in the same manner as the negative traits exercise in the previous chapter.

My Positive Tendencies   _____'s **Positive Tendencies**

As with the previous exercise, you will discover areas where you are alike and areas where you are different, areas where you agree and areas where you disagree. All of these can become strengths within your marriage if you approach them in the proper spirit.

I have listed below actual positive traits or behaviors that participants in my marriage encounter seminars have listed. Perhaps some of them will appear on your list for yourself or your partner.

POSITIVE TRAITS OR BEHAVIOR

Intelligent

Great family

Very forgiving

Nurturing

Loves God

Positive

Excellent work ethic

Strong morals

Good listener

Gorgeous

Good looks

Loving person

Loves children

Independent

Generous

Good at expressing self

Upbeat

Hard-working

Plans for the future

Great cook

Handsome

Likes to cuddle

Romantic

Considerate

Strong convictions

Artistic

Sense of style

Caring

Friendly

Compassionate

Carefree

Neatness of the home

Expressive

Organized

Good listener

Gentle

Giving

Attentive

Not lazy

Protective

Admits mistakes

Patient

Not critical

Open to new ideas

A wonderful dresser

Cute

Realistic

Sincere

Can keep a secret

Thrifty

Thoughtful

Has a quiet side

Not afraid of intimacy

Great personality

Spontaneous

Supportive

Exercises and works out

Optimistic

Adventurous

Extremely loyal

Creative

Confident

Trusting

Stable

Outgoing

Personal neatness

Personal grooming

Not shy

Articulate

Funny and humorous

Kind

Not selfish

Ambitious

Observant

Talented

Volunteers to help

Not judgmental

Flexible

Has a good heart

Motivated

Spunky

Practical

Courteous

Reliable

Helps in the kitchen

Financially responsible

Affectionate

Beautiful

Full of life

Adaptable to change

Lives by the rules

Conscious of health

Happy and bubbly
Good host/hostess
Respectful of others
Tender
Sensitive to my needs
Diligent
Good mechanic
Good fix-it person
Good with needle & thread
Their eyes
Their feet
Not cruel
Not deceitful
Well-liked
Not conceited
Not all drama

Gracious
Entertaining
Uses credit cards wisely
Keeps checkbook balanced
Pays bills on time
Versatile skills
Good carpenter
Artistic skills
Their hands
Their hair
Their laugh
Not mean-spirited
Smart
Popular
Not arrogant

That's quite a list of real positives that have been shared in my seminars. Positives are real, and we all have them. By gently encouraging one another, we can acquire new positives, and the positives we already have can grow and deepen. As we get to know who our partner really is behind their mask, we can become more tender and sensitive to them and more supportive of them.

Marriage is for a lifetime—and beyond. The Orthodox Church teaches that marriage, as a sacrament, is eternal. As a popular song some years back asked, "If love is not forever, then what's forever for?"

With each passing year it should become more obvious that the two of you are good for each other. Your marriage has created an environment that is healthy and affirming for both of you. With each passing year, your negatives begin to fade away and your positives deepen and increase in number. Let our love for each other give us the courage to learn how to care for and to cherish this one who knows us best and loves us most.

I have already mentioned several romantic comedies containing scenes that illustrate universal moments in developing human relationships. There is a great correlation between dating and romantic comedies. In romantic comedies we watch other people meet, be attracted to each other, have conflicts, ultimately find happiness in each other's arms, and (we want to believe) live happily ever after.

Dating is like a casting call in which we are the director looking for actors to be in our film. We have already cast ourselves as the perfect wife (or husband). We are now looking for just the right person to cast as our perfect husband (or wife) in our movie. After dating several people (casting calls) we have found the perfect one. They are now cast as our perfect husband/wife in our movie, *My Perfect Marriage*.

Below is a script of a few scenes from one couple's *My Perfect Marriage*.

SCENES FROM "MY PERFECT MARRIAGE"

RESTAURANT PARKING LOT—EARLY EVENING

Perfect Husband and Perfect Wife walk silently across the parking lot to their car. He unlocks the car with remote control. She lets herself in on the passenger side while he slides behind the wheel.

CAR INTERIOR—EARLY EVENING

As they drive away from the restaurant, Perfect Husband turns the car stereo on and inserts a CD. Simon & Garfunkel's "Like a Bridge over Troubled Water" begins to play. Perfect Wife stares silently out the window. Perfect Husband reaches forward and turns the car stereo off.

PERFECT HUSBAND
    Are you angry?

PERFECT WIFE
(*icily*)
    No.

PERFECT HUSBAND
    Are you upset?

PERFECT WIFE
(curtly)
> No.

Perfect Husband punches the car stereo back on.

CAR EXTERIOR—EARLY EVENING

Car is seen traveling down the road.

(VOICE OVER)
SIMON & GARFUNKEL SING
> Like a bridge over troubled water, I will lay me down.
> Like a bridge over troubled water, I will lay me down.

Car continues down road and turns into a driveway.

HOME EXTERIOR—EVENING

Perfect Wife gets out of car, slams door, and storms into the house. Perfect Husband follows her.

HOME INTERIOR—LATE EVENING

PERFECT HUSBAND
> Are you ready to talk now?

PERFECT WIFE
> Maybe.

PERFECT HUSBAND
> What did I do to make you so angry?

PERFECT WIFE
> I told you I wasn't angry.

PERFECT HUSBAND
> Okay. What did I do to upset you?

PERFECT WIFE
   I'm not upset.

PERFECT HUSBAND
   Okay, you're something. What did I do to make you feel what you're
   feeling right now?

PERFECT WIFE
(quietly)
   You hurt me . . .

PERFECT HUSBAND
stares silently.

PERFECT WIFE
   . . . I'm not angry. I'm hurt.

PERFECT HUSBAND
   What did I do that hurt you?

PERFECT WIFE
   You wouldn't share your meal with me.

PERFECT HUSBAND
   What?

PERFECT WIFE
   When I reached across to get a bite from your plate, you pushed my
   hand away.

PERFECT HUSBAND
   You're upset about that?

PERFECT WIFE
   I'm not upset. I'm hurt. There's a difference.

PERFECT HUSBAND

Oh yeah? They look the same to me.

PERFECT WIFE

When I'm hurt, I'm quiet. When I'm angry, I yell and throw things. Believe me, you'll know the difference. *(shakes her finger at him)* And if you don't shut up, you'll find out the difference right now.

HOME EXTERIOR—NIGHT

(VOICE OVER)
SIMON & GARFUNKEL SING

Like a bridge over troubled water, I will lay me down.
Like a bridge over troubled water, I will lay me down.

INSPIRATIONS TEA PARLOR—INTERIOR—DAY

Perfect Wife is having coffee and cake with her friend Tammy. They each have a coffee but are sharing a large slice of Bavarian Crème Chocolate Cake on a single plate set between them.

TAMMY

Sounds like a tough night. What started it?

PERFECT WIFE

We went to Avanti's. We were having a lovely dinner with nice wine. I had the roast duck with cherry sauce. He had a grilled rib eye that smelled wonderful. Without even thinking about it, I reached over with my fork to taste his steak.

TAMMY

So how was it?

PERFECT WIFE

How should I know? You'd have thought I broke all ten of the commandments at once!

Both use their forks at the same time to get another bite of cake from the same plate.

TAMMY

Neanderthals, I tell you, Neanderthals!

PERFECT WIFE

I've never been so hurt or felt so alone.

TAMMY

He kept you out, cut you off, and excluded you. *(She squeezes Perfect Wife's hand)* I'm so sorry. That had to hurt.

CHARLESTON'S RESTAURANT—INTERIOR—DAY

Perfect Husband and John are having hamburgers for lunch.

JOHN

My God, man, you can't win for losing.

PERFECT HUSBAND

We're at Avanti's. She's having the roast duck, and I'm having a steak. Out of nowhere she reaches across with her fork to get a bite of my steak.

JOHN

Oh my God, she can't do that. Doesn't she know you can't break that rule?

PERFECT HUSBAND

There's two things you can never do.

JOHN

Touch my girl and touch my food.

PERFECT HUSBAND

I was a freshman pledge sitting across the table from one of the old men. It looked like he had finished eating, and there was a whole piece of meat left he hadn't touched. I reached over with my fork and said, "If you're not going to . . ." Pow! He stabbed me in the back of my hand with his fork and nailed me to the table. He looked me straight in the eye and said, "Kid, there's two things you can never do. Touch my girl and touch my food."

JOHN
It's a rule. It's like the Eleventh Commandment.

PERFECT HUSBAND
It *is* the Eleventh Commandment. You can't touch my wife. You can't touch my food.

What's going on here? Perfect Husband and Perfect Wife each have a script, but they do not have the same script. They both have a script called *My Perfect Marriage*. But he has a script called *My Perfect Marriage* that he wrote, and she has a script called *My Perfect Marriage* that she wrote. They think they have the same script, but they don't. They have two different scripts with the same name.

In his script, the Perfect Wife knows the rule and would never touch the food on his plate. In her script, the Perfect Husband loves the intimacy of sharing their food and eating from one plate. The problem is not caused by either one being deceitful or contrary. The problem comes from having two different scripts of what each expects the other to say and do.

The above little script is, of course, fiction. But it is based on a telltale subtheme that runs throughout the movie *Made of Honor*, starring Patrick Dempsey and Michelle Monaghan, who play Tom and Hannah. The audience knows they are "right" for each other because they continually eat off each other's plates. Through the twists of the movie, Hannah gets engaged to Colin (Kevin McKidd). That Hannah is making a mistake in marrying Colin is confirmed to the audience when Colin rebuffs her when she tries to eat off his plate. Eventually the engagement is called off, and Hannah marries Tom instead.

In order for a couple to have the same script, either he must throw his script away and follow her script, or she must throw her script away and follow his. In either case, one has lost their personal identity and become only an actor in someone else's play. In a successful marriage, both must abandon their preconceived scripts. They must take a blank stack of paper and begin writing a brand new script written by the two of them together. Their new script is called *Our Perfect Marriage.*

The conflict in the above fictional script is real, but it does not have to be an ultimate threat to the couple's marriage. If such basic disagreements continue, the couple might conclude they are incompatible and head to divorce court. But often what couples think is incompatibility is nothing more than having different scripts. It is their scripts that are incompatible, not they themselves.

Building a strong marriage takes more than strong bricks and strong positive characteristics. The two of you must agree on what kind of house you are going to build together. Will it be a log home, a one-story ranch home, a two-story home, or a home with a basement? You must begin to agree on the common details of your life together.

Not every detail can be agreed on in advance. Life is lived day by day, and relationships grow and develop day by day. Your script of *Our Perfect Marriage* does not yet exist. You will create it as you go. You must recognize when conflicts between you are really only differences in your scripts. You and your partner simply have different opinions of what you expect from each other in a particular situation. When conflicts arise, it's time to talk about it, and the two of you write a new page for your marriage script.

The following exercise will give us an opportunity to work on learning how to agree with our partner.

In Palestine, where I am from, our roofs have four sides that slope together until they almost meet at the top. But instead of a peak, we build a flat square or rectangle at the very top center of the roof. This square or rectangle acts the same way a keystone does in an arch. It holds the roof together, so that its weight supports itself.

This kind of roof is a metaphor for this exercise. The flat center is God, who holds the home together. The four sides are four categories or divisions of life: *time, sacrifice, love,* and *discipline.*

Let me take a moment to define these four words.

- ✑ **Time:** By this I mean making time for each other a priority: time to shop, time to run errands together, time for conversation, listening, even being quiet together.

- ✑ **Love:** You will stay together no matter what. Your love is unconditional. You're permanently "hooked" on each other.

- ✑ **Sacrifice:** The willingness to give up personal preferences, habits, plans, quirks for your spouse. It's the martyrdom element of marriage where self-will places second.

- ✑ **Discipline:** Doing things right, paying the bills on time, picking up socks from the bedroom floor, arriving places on time, changing the oil and filter on your car, mowing the lawn.

Just above these four words in the exercise you'll find a list of words. Each word is to be placed under one of the four categories. Together you are to decide where each word goes. There are no right or wrong answers. There is only your mutual agreement that this is where you will place each word.

You are not randomly sorting the words into four categories. Talk together about the first word. Each word may have an intellectual meaning that we can find in a dictionary, but it also has an emotional meaning. There is an emotional connection between a word and the category you believe it should be in. Talk about what the category means to you in terms of your relationship and marriage. Share why you think the word connects best with this category rather than one of the others.

If you do come across a word you have difficulty agreeing on, go on to the next word. You can come back to that word at the end of the exercise.

Remember the purpose of this exercise is to practice learning how to agree. Both of you must participate. One of you can't do all the work, and the other just go along with it. Both of you must equally participate and share what these words mean to you in terms of your relationship and marriage.

EXERCISE 3

AGREEING ON A COMMON VISION

Decide together which of the four categories listed at the end each word will go in.

Equality	Expectation	Compassion
Mentoring	Rules	Availability
Attention	Pride	Providing
Constancy	Commitment	Finance
Humility	Prayer	Fellowship
Priority	Accountability	Monetary
Sharing	Boundaries	Language
Temperate	Admission	Responsibility
Encouragement	Time Out	Positive
Over-indulging	Limited Choices	Safety
Freedom	Power/Control	Rights
Unconditional	Educate	Supervise
Negative	Standard Right/Wrong	

FOUR CATEGORIES OR PARTS OF OUR ROOF

Time	Love	Sacrifice	Discipline
_____	_____	_____	_____
_____	_____	_____	_____
_____	_____	_____	_____
_____	_____	_____	_____
_____	_____	_____	_____
_____	_____	_____	_____
_____	_____	_____	_____
_____	_____	_____	_____
_____	_____	_____	_____
_____	_____	_____	_____

_____ _____ _____ _____
_____ _____ _____ _____
_____ _____ _____ _____

EXERCISE 4

ACHIEVING A SHARED VISION

The King James Version of Amos 3:3 asks, "Can two walk together except they be agreed?" We cannot walk together on the journey of life unless we have agreed on a time and place to meet. We must agree on the direction we're going to take.

One of the most important, yet seldom talked about, issues of marriage is the vision you share for your relationship. As you begin this journey of life, where are you headed? What is the destination of your relationship?

Highway I-35 runs north and south through Oklahoma. If a couple wants to go to Dallas for the weekend, they must go south on the interstate. If they want to go to Wichita, they must go north. If you've chosen to go to Dallas, there are major markers that indicate you are correctly headed south. You will pass through Moore, Norman, Purcell, Paul's Valley, and Ardmore before crossing into Texas at Gainesville. If, however, you pass through Guthrie, the Stillwater exit, Perry, Tonkawa, and Ponca City, then you're headed to Kansas instead of Texas.

Take a moment to discuss together markers on your journey that will let you know you're headed in the right direction. Where would you like your relationship to be in three months, seven months, twelve months? Where do you hope to be as a couple? Consider communication and conflict, spirituality, intimacy, financial management, outside relationships, traditions for holidays, and so on. Be as specific as possible.

Our goals at three months:

_____
_____
_____

_____
_____
_____

Our goals at seven months:

_____
_____
_____
_____
_____
_____
_____

Our goals at twelve months:

_____
_____
_____
_____
_____
_____

What are some of the roadblocks that could prevent us from meeting these goals?

_____
_____
_____
_____
_____
_____
_____
_____
_____

AGES AND STAGES OF LIFE

Each of us looks at life through our own eyes. Different people will see the same event differently. That is obvious. What is not so obvious is that within age groups, people often view events from the same perspective. People inside an age group will see life pretty much the same way, but differently from those in a different age group. Let me illustrate this with two pieces that circulated on the internet.

The first piece contains a list of the desirable qualities a woman might look for in a man. But notice how those qualities change depending on which age group is being asked!

WHAT I WANT IN A MAN

Original List (age 22)
- Handsome
- Charming
- Financially successful
- A caring listener
- Witty
- In good shape
- Dresses with style
- Appreciates finer things
- Full of thoughtful surprises

Revised List (age 32)

- ∞ Nice-looking
- ∞ Opens car doors, holds chairs
- ∞ Has enough money for a nice dinner
- ∞ Listens more than talks
- ∞ Laughs at my jokes
- ∞ Carries bags of groceries with ease
- ∞ Owns at least one tie
- ∞ Appreciates a good home-cooked meal
- ∞ Remembers birthdays and anniversaries

Revised List (age 42)

- ∞ Not too ugly
- ∞ Doesn't drive off until I'm in the car
- ∞ Works steadily—splurges on dinner out occasionally
- ∞ Nods head when I'm talking
- ∞ Usually remembers punch lines of jokes
- ∞ Is in good enough shape to rearrange the furniture
- ∞ Wears a shirt that covers his stomach
- ∞ Knows not to buy champagne with screw-top lids
- ∞ Remembers to put the toilet seat down
- ∞ Shaves most weekends

Revised List (age 52)

- ∞ Keeps hair in nose and ears trimmed
- ∞ Doesn't belch or scratch in public
- ∞ Doesn't borrow money too often
- ∞ Doesn't nod off to sleep when I'm venting
- ∞ Doesn't retell the same joke too many times
- ∞ Is in good enough shape to get off the couch on weekends
- ∞ Usually wears matching socks and fresh underwear
- ∞ Appreciates a good TV dinner
- ∞ Remembers my name on occasion
- ∞ Shaves some weekends

Revised List (age 62)
- Doesn't scare small children
- Remembers where the bathroom is
- Doesn't require much money for upkeep
- Only snores lightly when asleep
- Remembers why he's laughing
- Is in good enough shape to stand up by himself
- Usually wears some clothes
- Likes soft foods
- Remembers where he left his teeth
- Remembers that it's the weekend

Revised List (age 72)
- Breathing
- Doesn't miss the toilet

The second piece circulating on the internet is about changing realities for men.

A group of 40-year-old buddies discuss and discuss where they should meet for dinner. Finally it is agreed that they should meet at the Gasthof zum Loewen restaurant because the waitresses are pretty.

Ten years later, at 50 years of age, the group meets again, and once again they discuss and discuss where they should meet. Finally it is agreed that they should meet at the Gasthof zum Loewen because the food there is very good and the wine selection is good also.

Ten years later, at 60 years of age, the group meets again and once again they discuss and discuss where they should meet. Finally it is agreed that they should meet at the Gasthof zum Loewen because they can eat there in peace and quiet and the restaurant is smoke-free.

Ten years later, at 70 years of age, the group meets again and once again they discuss and discuss where they should meet. Finally it is agreed that they should meet at the Gasthof zum Loewen because the restaurant is wheelchair accessible and they even have an elevator.

Ten years later, at 80 years of age, the group meets again and once again they discuss and discuss where they should meet. Finally it is agreed that they should meet at the Gasthof zum Loewen because they have never been there before.

Both of these articles are humorous ways of reminding us of our changing perspective throughout life. It is easy to be myopic and to view life only from the perspective of our present stage in life. It is true that we should live life one day at a time. However, there is a danger in being nearsighted: When we fail to see the larger picture, we will fail to anticipate the changing landscape of the future.

Many relationships may work for a moment in the present. Two people may seem so right for each other at this particular time and place in their lives. But our lives are more than this moment. It takes a special relationship to last a lifetime.

Life expectancies have changed throughout history, but the description given in Psalm 90:10 continues to be a good guide to go by: "The days of our lives *are* seventy years; / And if by reason of strength *they are* eighty years..." Some, of course, do not live to be seventy; because of medical technology and science others live much longer, perhaps even well into their nineties or beyond.

The span of life covers infancy, childhood, adolescence, young adulthood, and adulthood and encompasses many changes. But the span does not go on forever. Our days are numbered. We are all like the flowers that bloom and the grass that grows for a season and is gone. "All flesh *is* grass, / And all its loveliness *is* like the flower of the field. / The grass withers, the flower fades" (Isaiah 40:6–7).

Children and teenagers can't wait till they grow up. They want to date, drive, smoke, and drink alcoholic beverages. They are in a hurry to grow, and they think they will live forever. But the truth is, no one can add one iota to his life. "Which of you by worrying can add one cubit to his stature?" (Matthew 6:27).

Marriage is not just for the moment. Marriage is for the long haul. When the wedding is over, the marriage is just beginning. You and your spouse will age, grow, and mature. So will your marriage. Even as the two of you have chosen to be together during this stage of your life, you must continue to choose to remain together in the successive stages yet to come.

Another cute story making the rounds on the internet illustrates that life changes as we live it together.

> After being married for 40 years, I took a careful look at my wife one day and said, "Darling, 40 years ago we had a cheap apartment, a cheap car, slept on a sofa bed, and watched a 10-inch black-and-white TV, but I went to sleep every night with a hot 25-year-old girl. Now I have a $500,000 home, a $45,000 car, a nice big bed, and a plasma screen TV, but I'm sleeping with a 65-year-old woman. It seems to me that you're not holding up your side of things."
>
> My wife is a very reasonable woman. She told me to go out and find a hot 25-year-old gal, and she would make sure that I would once again be living in a cheap apartment, driving a cheap car, sleeping on a sofa bed, and watching a 10-inch black-and-white TV.
>
> Aren't older women great? They really know how to solve your mid-life crisis!

The man in the above story noticed that the external circumstances of his life had improved through the years. He also noticed that his wife had changed. She was not at 65 what she had been at 25. What he, of course, failed to notice was that he also had changed. He was not a young horse himself any longer. It is totally unrealistic to see ourselves as always being 25, and equally unrealistic to expect our spouse always to be 25. Like it or not, we will outgrow our present stage in life. The trick is to outgrow it together.

Couples celebrate their wedding anniversary every year. But there are three anniversaries that are particularly marked: the twenty-fifth, the fiftieth, and the seventy-fifth. In order to achieve these celebrations, a couple must have married young, have good health, and have mastered the art of becoming one. One thing is for certain—no couple celebrates these milestones by accident. Strong marriages don't just happen, nor do long marriages happen by default.

EXERCISE 5

OUR STAGE IN LIFE

On the scale below, write in your age on the top where it falls on the scale. On the bottom, write in the ages of your parents and your grandparents.

0   25   50   75+

If you are under age 25, then you have almost completed the first third of your life. If you are between 25 and 50, you are in the second stage of your life. If you are over 50, then you are now in the last stage of your journey. Whatever years come afterwards are a blessing from God.

While we like to think in terms of the biblical seventy years, the truth is that each of us is living on borrowed time. It is not enough to set out on a journey; we must anticipate the end of the journey as well. It is in thinking of death that we learn to appreciate life and have an opportunity to value time as a gift. Men and women must cherish their relationship today. We must not postpone taking care of each other and our relationship. The day will come when it will be too late.

In the Orthodox Faith we often speak about being on a journey, the journey of salvation. We are also on the journey of life. Jesus said there are many broad roads that people go speeding by on. These all look like good roads and promise to bring us to such wonderful destinations. But they are all dead-end roads. They lead to the destruction of our homes, our children, our families, and our marriages. But there is a small gate and a narrow path that does not have all the glamour and glitz of the broad way. And those who find this gate and follow this narrow path to the end will find life along the way, and the fullness of life waiting for them at the end (see Matthew 7:13–14).

On the journey of life we need a map, a plan of where we're headed and how we're going to get there. We must have an ongoing conversation with the map and with our traveling companion, lest we wake up and realize we took a wrong turn and have been going in the wrong direction.

Likewise, in our marriages, we must be conscious of and informed about the signs of life that tell us we're headed the wrong way. There are warning signs that, if ignored, can shake our marriage and hurl us off toward unknown and unintended destinations. But even when events have caused us to detour, or we have taken wrong turns, and we find ourselves going the wrong way on unknown roads, it is still possible to return to the right path.

Our marriages will go through challenges—many minor and some major. We will face obstacles and detours of all kinds—emotional, financial, health, external influences, extended family issues, as well as environmental circumstances (such as hating the place where you live).

These challenges, obstacles, and detours must not be ignored. You must find time as a couple to discuss them together and to seek the trusted counsel of others. If you want to protect your marriage, do not ignore these issues. If you want to save your marriage in the future, do not ignore your spouse now.

Problems will not go away by themselves. Marriage is not a bed of roses or a Walt Disney fairy tale with everyone living "happily ever after." Marriage requires working towards finding solutions to whatever life throws at you. It requires a commitment of love, devotion, and forgiveness between the two of you. You must believe, "We are in this together, and we're going to make it."

Our automobiles do not always start even though they have all the necessary technical elements. But we don't abandon our cars when they fail to start. We get help; we get the problem solved; and we continue on our way. Once our car is running again, it now depends on us how well we drive it and in what direction we take off.

Marriage requires daily maintenance. I must say it again: Do not take your spouse for granted. Do not take your marriage for granted.

Marriage is like a garden. If you want to eat from its harvest, you must till it, plant it, fertilize it, weed it, water it, and then harvest it. When you do so, you will experience the joy of creation as God intended it.

But it is not enough to do everything just mentioned. What if you have insects, animals, or birds eating your garden? You must defend and protect your garden from the things that want to destroy it. So you fence it; you guard it. You spray it and set up a scarecrow. You do what it takes to protect and defend your garden.

Your marriage is more precious than a garden. Many negative forces attack our marriages. We are surrounded by a culture that is hostile to marriage. Television, movies, and magazines all promote behaviors that will destroy our marriages if we engage in them. People with hidden agendas and hidden motives will seek to undermine the unity we have with our spouse. The seducer and the temptress, disguised as gentle friends, are secretly wolves patiently waiting to devour us.

Life is not static. Our marriages must not become static. Our spouses must grow, and we must grow. Holding hands, we can grow together. In marriage, we are embarking on the journey of life together. On this journey the scenery will change, the seasons will change, and we will change. But we can arrive at the end of our journey with our marriage intact, and even more in love than the day we got married.

COSTLY STONES &
STRONG FOUNDATIONS

Here in Oklahoma, much of our soil has red clay in it. Flying into Oklahoma City in the daytime, you can look out an airplane window and see how red the dirt is. Oklahoma mothers know it is almost impossible to get the red dirt stains out of white socks.

But not all of the soil is equally mixed with clay; there are variations. In the hot days of July and August, the dry Oklahoma soil can get deep cracks in it. These variations coupled with changing movements of the soil can cause the foundations of houses to shift and crack. Several major foundation repair companies advertise the advantages of their particular system in "putting your home back on a strong foundation."

It is equally important that our marriage and family are built on a deep and strong foundation. It is quite costly to come in later, after the house is built, to repair a faulty foundation. Similarly, it is only at great emotional expense, accompanied with great energy and effort, that the poor foundations of a marriage and family can be repaired.

We must realize that all foundations are not created equal. Jesus told a parable about two different kinds of foundation and what happens when we build on them.

> "Therefore whoever hears these sayings of Mine, and does them, I will liken him to a wise man who built his house on the rock: and the rain descended, the floods came, and the winds blew and beat on that house; and it did not fall, for it was founded on the rock.

"But everyone who hears these sayings of Mine, and does not do them, will be like a foolish man who built his house on the sand: and the rain descended, the floods came, and the winds blew and beat on that house; and it fell. And great was its fall." (Matthew 7:24–27)

In order for our marriages to survive the storms of life, we must be careful not to build our home on sand. A beach house may be a fun place to visit on a vacation, but it is an extremely dangerous place to live year after year. Storms come, the high tide pounds, the sand shifts, and hurricanes approach. Lives and marriages built on sand stand no more chance of surviving than sandcastles built on the shore at low tide. All it takes is one huge wave, and they are gone.

But homes built on a firm foundation have a better chance of surviving whatever storms life may bring. It is impossible to build too strong a foundation. Foundations that are dug deep and make use of concrete and reinforced steel increase the odds of the building's survival.

In his parable about building one's house on the sand, Jesus reminds us that not all building sites—not all philosophies of life and success—are equal. St. Luke's version of the parable reminds us that even good building sites require a strong foundation:

"Whoever comes to Me, and hears My sayings and does them, I will show you whom he is like: He is like a man building a house, who dug deep and laid the foundation on the rock. And when the flood arose, the stream beat vehemently against that house, and could not shake it, for it was founded on the rock. But he who heard and did nothing is like a man who built a house on the earth without a foundation, against which the stream beat vehemently; and immediately it fell. And the ruin of that house was great." (Luke 6:47–49)

It is not enough to build on firm ground instead of sand. It is important to put a strong foundation into the ground and to build a sturdy house upon it. Of particular importance when building a foundation are the corners, which carry the greatest load and anchor the structure. Good corners are dug deeper and wider than the rest of the foundation. Extra steel is used to reinforce the concrete there.

In the Old Testament, we are told that King Solomon built many buildings in Jerusalem, including the Holy Temple. Great care was taken in building the Temple foundation. Builders at that time did not have concrete and steel to use. Instead they quarried "large stones, costly stones, *and* hewn stones, to lay the foundation" of the Holy Temple (1 Kings 5:17 [3 Kg 6:2, OSB]).

In order for our homes and marriages to survive, we must quarry four great stones, gigantic stones that will anchor the four corners. Great stones do not come cheap. They are costly stones. They require an investment of time, energy, effort, and commitment. It took Solomon's men three years to quarry the gigantic costly stones for the foundation of the Holy Temple.

The four costly stones that will anchor your home, strengthen your relationship, and sustain your marriage are Love, Faith, Trust, and Forgiveness.

FIRST COSTLY STONE: LOVE

The first foundation cornerstone is love. In English we have only one word for love. But the Ancient Greeks thought love was more complicated. They created four terms to describe four different aspects of love.

Agape (αγαπε) is the love of God for mankind, a sacrificial love. This is the term used in John 3:16: "For God so loved (αγαπε) the world that He gave His only begotten Son, that whoever believes in Him should not perish but have everlasting life."

Philia (φιλια) is the term for the affection between friends. It includes loyalty to one's family and love of one's country. It is found in the terms *philosophy,* love of wisdom, and *philadelphia*, brotherly love. The third term, *eros* (εροσ), is passionate love, a romantic love filled with sensual desire and longing. This is the type of love we think of between husband and wife. And the fourth term is *storge* (στοργε). *Storge* is the love within a family, of parents for their children and children towards their parents.

Greek has four words, but in English we have the single term *love* that covers all four Greek terms. In English it is possible for two people to use the word *love* but not mean the same thing. Let me illustrate from a passage in the Bible.

In the Gospel of John, the risen Christ comes to Peter after Peter has denied him three times. In the English translation, Jesus asks Peter three times, "Peter, do you love Me?" Each time Peter says, "Yes." After the third time, Peter is saddened that Christ has asked him three times if he loves Him. The implication is that Christ did not believe him the first two times, so He has to ask yet a third time whether Peter loves Him. Also implied is that Christ asks him three times because Peter denied Him three times.

But in the Greek New Testament, the story reads much differently. Jesus asks Peter, "Do you *agape* Me?" Peter replies, "Yes, Lord, I *philia* You." A second time Jesus asks Peter, "Do you *agape* Me?" A second time Peter replies, "Yes, Lord, I *philia* You." But the third time Jesus asks, "Peter, do you *philia* Me?" Peter is saddened that the third time Christ asks him if he feels *philia* for Him. It is not the fact that Christ asks him three times that saddens Peter. It is the fact that the third time, Christ uses the word *philia* instead of *agape*.

An English reader misses the real point of the passage; having only one word for love, an English reader assumes the term means the same each time it is used. Couples can miss the real message in their relationships as well. A husband and wife can say "I love you" to each other and not mean the same thing.

Social psychologist John A. Lee saw in the Greek terms four different approaches to love itself. Lee identified six primary love theories or "colors" that define different ways people fall in love and speak of love.[5] Each color represents a different approach that people use in their interpersonal relationships. His six categories are explained below.

Eros—erotic, passionate, sensual, and physical love that is the basis for romantic love.

> People who fall into this category believe in love at first sight. Marriage to them is an extended honeymoon in which they call each other "sweetheart" or "honey."

Ludus—love that is played as a game or sport.

> People in this category play the field seeking conquests. They see marriage as a trap and are likely to be unfaithful.

---

5   John A. Lee, *The Colors of Love: an exploration of the ways of loving* (New York: New Press, 1973)

Storge—an affectionate love that slowly develops from friendship.

> This type categorizes best friends who eventually fall in love, or people in love who eventually become best friends. There is great sharing between the two, but often a lack of passion.

Pragma—a love that is pragmatic, head-driven and not heart-driven.

> People in this category are practical lovers. They select a partner by using a shopping list and marry the one who has the most to offer them. They carefully weigh and calculate the rewards and costs of a relationship.

Mania—an obsessive and highly volatile love.

> People who love this way are the possessive ones. Their "need" drives them into a relationship. Marriage is seen as ownership and children as competitors for the spouse's time, attention, and money. These are the desperately jealous ones.

Agape—a selfless, altruistic love; a spiritual, sacrificial love.

> People in this category are the self-sacrificing, long-suffering ones. They tend to be spiritual or religious. Sex is seen as a gift between two people, and children are a sacred trust. Without a proper balance, agape love can become martyrdom: "I would rather suffer than have my partner (or my children) suffer."

Who would ever have guessed that people who are dating might be thinking of love in six entirely different ways! No wonder love is complicated and human relationships take work.

Clyde and Susan Hendrick expanded the work begun by Lee, calling the six categories "love styles." They found that people are drawn to others with a similar love style and that relationships based on similar love styles last longer. They developed a Love Attitude Scale that has proved useful to couples in discovering each other's love style or approach to love. Many of the online dating services make use of different versions of the categories created by Lee and expanded by the Hendricks.

The Love Attitude Scale is a useful and fun way of discovering our own basic approach to love and what we mean by the term "love." It also gives us an insight into our partner's way of understanding love, and what they mean when they say the word "love."

EXERCISE 6

LOVE ATTITUDE SCALE[6]

Listed below are several statements that reflect different attitudes about love. For each statement, fill in the blank using the response that indicates how much you agree or disagree with that statement.

Whenever possible, answer the questions with your spouse or fiancé(e) in mind. There are no right or wrong answers; we each carry traits from the different styles of love. For each question, score the following on the line for each statement:

(1) Strongly agree

(2) Moderately agree

(3) Neutral—neither agree nor disagree

(4) Moderately disagree

(5) Strongly disagree

LOVE STYLE A

_____ My partner and I were attracted to each other immediately after we first met.

_____ My partner and I have the right physical chemistry between us.

_____ Our relationship is intense and satisfying.

_____ I feel that my partner and I were meant for each other.

_____ My partner and I became emotionally involved rather quickly.

_____ My partner and I really understand each other.

_____ My partner fits my ideal standards for physical beauty/handsomeness.

LOVE STYLE B

_____ I try to keep my partner a little uncertain about my commitment to him/her.

---

6 Love Attitude Scale adapted from: http://iws.ccccd.edu/emcdonald/human sexuality/Handouts_to_download/Love Attitudes Scale-Chapter 7.htm on 10/04/05. C. Hendrick & S.S. Hendrick (1990). A relationship-specific version of the Love Attitude Scale, *Journal of Social Behavior and Personality*, 5, 239–254.

_____ I believe that what my partner does not know about me won't hurt him/her.

_____ I have sometimes had to keep my partner from finding out about other partners.

_____ I could get over my affair with my partner pretty easily and quickly.

_____ My partner would get upset if he/she knew some of the things I've done with others.

_____ When my partner gets too dependent on me, I want to back off a little.

_____ I enjoy playing the game of love with my partner and a number of other partners.

LOVE STYLE C

_____ It is hard for me to say exactly when our friendship turned into love.

_____ To be genuine, our love first required caring for a while.

_____ I expect to always be friends with my partner.

_____ Our love is the best kind because it grew out of a long friendship.

_____ Our friendship merged gradually into love over time.

_____ Our love is really a deep friendship, not a mysterious, mystical emotion.

_____ Our love relationship is the most satisfying because it developed from a good friendship.

LOVE STYLE D

_____ I considered what my partner was going to become in life before I committed myself to him/her.

_____ I tried to plan my life carefully before choosing my partner.

_____ In choosing my partner, I believe it was best to love someone with a similar background.

_____ A main consideration in choosing my partner was how he/she would reflect on my family.

_____ An important factor in choosing my partner was whether or not he/she would be a good parent.

_____ One consideration in choosing my partner was how he/she would reflect on my career.

_____ Before getting very involved with my partner, I tried to figure out how compatible his/her hereditary background would be with mine in case we ever had children.

LOVE STYLE E

_____ When things are not right with my partner and me, my stomach gets upset.

_____ If my partner and I broke up, I would get so depressed that I would even think of suicide.

_____ Sometimes I get so excited about being in love with my partner that I cannot sleep.

_____ When my partner does not pay attention to me, I feel sick all over.

_____ Since I have been in love with my partner, I have had trouble concentrating on anything else.

_____ I cannot relax if I suspect that my partner is with someone else.

_____ If my partner ignores me for a while, I sometimes do stupid things to try to get his/her attention back.

LOVE STYLE F

_____ I try to always help my partner through difficult times.

_____ I would rather suffer myself than let my partner suffer.

_____ I cannot be happy unless I place my partner's happiness before my own.

_____ I am usually willing to sacrifice my own wishes to let my partner achieve his/hers.

_____ Whatever I own is my partner's to use as he/she chooses.

_____ When my partner gets angry with me, I still love him/her fully and unconditionally.

_____ I would endure all things for the sake of my partner.

To determine your "score," after both of you have marked your answers from 1–5 on each line, go back and add your individual answers for each Love Style. Write your Love Style Totals below.

	Her Love Style Totals	His Love Style Totals
Love Style A	_____	_____
Love Style B	_____	_____
Love Style C	_____	_____
Love Style D	_____	_____
Love Style E	_____	_____
Love Style F	_____	_____

Your point range for each Love Style is 7–35. The lower the number, the more strongly you identify with a particular Love Style.

What did you learn about yourself? About your spouse? Are you surprised at what you learned? Below I have identified each Love Style with a description for each one. Do these descriptions fit you? Are they partially correct? Or do they miss the boat completely?

THE SIX LOVE TYPES[7]

LOVE STYLE A: EROS

The Eros lover is characterized by passion, though a passion broader than just a physical one. The Eros lover tends to be drawn toward a preferred physical type, and thus there may be an immediate recognition or "aha" when meeting a potential love partner. This lover is intense and wants to be involved with a partner on all levels, becoming physically affectionate (and intimate), talking for hours, and learning all about the partner. The Eros lover is fully and openly "present," is self-confident and trusting, and balances intensity with an appropriate sense of boundaries.

---

7 Adapted from Hendrick, Susan S., "Close Relationships Research: A Resource for Couple and Family Therapists," *Journal of Marital and Family Therapy*, Jan 2004; retrieved from http://findarticles.com/p/articles/mi_qa3658/is_200401/ai_n9350166/pg_5, on 04/09/08.

LOVE STYLE B: LUDUS

The Ludus lover, in contrast, is not interested in intensity, but rather experiences love as a game to be played for mutual enjoyment but not necessarily with any serious outcome in mind. Ludic lovers do not have a preferred physical type. Although ludic lovers may be in a partnered relationship with someone, ludic love is best played with several partners at a time, so that different people may be enjoyed for different qualities, in different activities, with no one person or relationship taking precedence over another. A ludic lover may hurt a partner inadvertently, but the goal is to enjoy relationships with a variety of people, with everyone having fun and no one getting hurt.

LOVE STYLE C: STORGE

"The Storge lover is someone who builds a love relationship on a strong base of friendship. The goal is: a companionable, secure, trusting relationship with a partner who is similar in terms of attitudes and values. This similarity is much more important to Storge than physical appearance or sexual satisfaction because this orientation to love is more likely to seek long-term commitment rather than short-term excitement."[8]

LOVE STYLE D: PRAGMA

The Pragma lover is all that the name implies, including practical and pragmatic. A Pragma lover may or may not have a preferred physical type, but he or she will surely have a virtual (or actual) shopping list of qualities sought in a partner. This type of lover may profit from working with a matchmaker or a computer dating service, in which inappropriate relationship candidates will be screened out. "The pragmatic lover isn't looking for great excitement and drama, but, rather, for a suitable partner with whom a satisfying, rewarding life can be built."[9]

LOVE STYLE E: MANIA

The manic lover is also aptly characterized by the love style name, in that emotional highs and lows, as well as dependence, possessiveness, jealousy,

---

8 S. Hendrick & Hendrick, 1992, p. 65.

9 S. Hendrick & Hendrick, 1992, p. 66.

and insecurity are typically present. A manic lover yearns for a love relationship but finds it elusive, because she or he seems compelled to push for commitment from a partner, does not really trust the commitment even if it is forthcoming, and is always afraid that the partner will find someone else. Another aspect of mania is physical symptoms, such as difficulty eating or sleeping. Overall, the manic lover always seems to be looking for the cloud around the silver lining.

LOVE STYLE F: AGAPE

The Agape lover is the rarest type. Agape is characterized by altruism, such that the partner's welfare is more important than one's own, and what one can give in a relationship is more important than what one gets. Indeed, Agape has much in common with compassionate love. The idealism of Agape means that there is no one preferred physical type in a partner, and indeed, sensuality and sexuality are likely to be much less important than more spiritual qualities. Although pure Agape is unlikely to exist on the physical plane of this world, **agapic qualities are extremely important as relationships encounter inevitable ups and downs.**

Obviously no one is exclusively one love type or love style. We are complex people, and we are always more than a number. Numbers can be helpful, however. Knowing what time it is, or how much time you have left to complete an exam, or how much further it is to the destination is helpful because these things let us know where we are on a scale. Am I closer to this part of the scale or to that part? Am I in the middle or close to the end?

Orthodox Christians approach life from the point of view of mystery. We can quantify certain things about ourselves (such as height, weight, blood pressure, and age); nonetheless, we can never be reduced to a number. Even as the Trinity is a mystery, so too is each one of us. We can explain biological sexuality and sexual attraction. But we cannot explain love. Love—the relationship of a man and a woman that transcends sexual mating—is a mystery. Proverbs declares:

> There are three *things which* are too wonderful for me,
> Yes, four *which* I do not understand:

The way of an eagle in the air,

The way of a serpent on a rock,

The way of a ship in the midst of the sea,

And the way of a man with a virgin. (Proverbs 30:18–19)

Science may give us answers to the first three. But the relationship of men and women is still a mystery.

God created us male and female. Unlike the animals, we were created for relationships. A few species may mate for life, but we are the only species that has not only the relationship of husband and wife for a lifetime, but the relationship of parent and child for a lifetime as well. We are the only species with grandparents.

God said that it is not good for us to be alone. We were created male and female for sexual companionship and relationship. Our relationships spring from our God-given human need. Just as God blessed Adam and Eve in the Garden of Eden, so He has created all mankind to be blessed by having a companion.

SECOND COSTLY STONE: FAITH

The second foundation cornerstone is faith. Having faith in God trains us to have faith also in our partner. Having faith in God is more than believing that God exists. It means you trust God to be and do all that He says He is and will do. St. Paul put it this way: "I know whom I have believed and am persuaded that He is able to keep what I have committed to Him until that Day" (2 Timothy 1:12).

A wedding is only the beginning of your life together. Your whole future as a couple awaits you. Because you have gotten to know each other, you now believe this person is the partner for you—not only the one for you today, but the one for you in all the tomorrows in front of you. You are saying, "I believe in *us*. I believe in you and will guard your heart. And I believe that you will guard my heart as well."

Your relationship with God as a couple is important. The more your faith in God as a couple grows, the stronger your faith in each other becomes. Building your relationship requires a willingness to talk about your faith in God. You both may not be at the same place in your relationship with God.

But when you talk about your faith (or your lack of faith) and accept each other where you are, your faith in God as a couple will begin to grow. As you exercise your faith together, you will discover your faith in each other will grow as well.

On more than one occasion, as He brought healing to a person, Christ said, "Your faith has made you well."[10] Your faith in your partner and in your marriage can heal rough spots that may arise in your relationship.

Make no mistake. Satan is always trying to disrupt and destroy not only your life but also your faith—your faith in God and your faith in each other. There is a relationship between faith and marriage. When you lose your faith, your marriage will begin to decline. So constantly pray and ask God to strengthen your faith in Him and in each other.

It takes faith to reveal who you are to your partner. You have to believe that he or she will not betray you. Remember the Johari Window. In marriage we choose to reveal more of who we are to our spouse. We will reveal some things that we know about ourselves, but we will also reveal things we don't realize about ourselves. With this one special person, we have chosen to risk being caught in the act of being who we are in the privacy of our relationship together.

This is why being unfaithful strikes at the heart of a relationship. Being unfaithful is a betrayal of the very foundation of the relationship because it repudiates the exclusivity and uniqueness of this one special relationship. Being unfaithful really declares that a marriage relationship is nothing more than just one among other relationships that one may choose to have simultaneously.

In the movie *You've Got Mail*, both Kathleen Kelly (played by Meg Ryan) and Joe Fox (played by Tom Hanks) are unfaithful to their respective live-in partners. They are not having a real affair with someone else, but they are having an emotional affair with each other on the internet. It is obvious that neither treats their live-in relationship as a unique and categorically different (and therefore exclusive) kind of relationship. In fact, the audience is not quite sure what their expectations are of their already-living-together relationship. But at the very least, it is obvious in this movie, and almost

10 See for example Matthew 9:22, 29; Mark 5:34; 10:52; Luke 7:50; 8:48; 17:19; 18:42.

all movies with live-in relationships, that such relationships never possess built-in exclusivity. At least in the movies, both partners are free to explore and engage in other mutually fulfilling relationships.

Both Kathleen and Joe wait till their live-in partners are out of the apartment before they sneak online to see if their secret online "special friend" has sent them mail. Eventually their online unfaithfulness causes them to detach themselves emotionally from their partners. Meanwhile, their partners likewise have been drawn to someone new and soon move out. Kathleen and Joe are now free to take their online emotional attachment offline and into the real world, where all human relationships must eventually be lived.

But what rules exist now for Kathleen and Joe? What makes their new real relationship somehow categorically different from their online cheating relationship? What makes it different from their old real relationship? Does this new relationship now possess exclusivity? If so, what gives it its exclusivity? Without a conscious acceptance and commitment to exclusivity, what keeps them from repeating their past behavior of seeking new emotional attachments with new secret online partners?

You've Got Mail ends without telling us what kind of relationship Kathleen and Joe have in the real world. Will they move in together and be just live-in partners? If so, then the only thing that has happened in this movie is that one set of live-in partners has been replaced by a new set.

But you, the audience, object that their new relationship is different. Kathleen and Joe really love each other, you say, and they didn't really love their old partners. Therefore it is real love, you say, that makes the difference.

Another Meg Ryan and Tom Hanks film, *Sleepless in Seattle*, tells us the difference "is magic." In that movie Annie (Meg Ryan) ditches her live-in partner because she's looking for a relationship with magic, something she realizes her present relationship lacks. Annie takes off running to find Sam (Tom Hanks) and his son, Jonah.

Both *Sleepless in Seattle* and *You've Got Mail* tell the same story and end the same way. Never does Tom Hanks' character ask, "Will you marry me?" Are we in the audience supposed to believe that, since Kathleen and Joe love each other and Annie and Sam have magic, they will not cheat on each other the way they did on their former partners? It may work in the movies. In fairy tales people may live "happily ever after," but not in real life.

It is only marriage that changes things. By getting married, Annie/Kathleen and Sam/Joe would be declaring that this relationship is somehow categorically different from all other relationships.

By being faithful to each other, we declare that marriage is an exclusive relationship. "Therefore a man shall leave his father and mother and be joined to his wife, and they shall become one flesh" (Genesis 2:24). In many Western weddings the bride and groom vow "to forsake all others and to cling only unto each other as long as we both shall live." By being faithful, we guard the uniqueness of our relationship by guarding each other with a love demonstrated by our faithfulness.

The marriage relationship is exclusive. This does not mean that other, secondary relationships do not exist. Our parents continue to be part of our lives, and so do our friends. But a man's wife always comes before his mother and father or any friend, male or female. Likewise a woman's husband always comes before any parent or friend.

There may be, and can be, many secondary relationships, but there can only be one primary relationship. Marriage requires us to acknowledge that this relationship is of a different kind from all others. Other relationships may call on us to be loyal, but marriage transcends all other relationships and requires that our loyalty to our spouse be transformed into being faithful.

THIRD COSTLY STONE: TRUST

The third cornerstone of a strong marriage foundation is trust. Trust is the nuts and bolts of a relationship.

We mentioned earlier the passage from the Book of Amos: "Can two walk together unless they are agreed?" (Amos 3:3 KJV). In order to walk together, we must first agree to meet. We must agree on what day, what time, and where to meet. It is impossible to go on a date without these points of agreement. Once they are settled, we trust the other person to keep each of the points of agreement of day, time, and place. If they do, our trust has been validated, and we see the other person as trustworthy.

There is nothing worse than the loneliness, abandonment, and embarrassment of waiting for someone who does not show. The theme of a missed appointment, of being "stood up," made a key turning point in the movie *An*

Affair to Remember, starring Cary Grant and Deborah Kerr. Deborah Kerr's character (through no fault of her own) failed to keep her appointment to meet Grant on top of the Empire State Building. This film scenario underscores our basic instinct: You can't trust someone who stands you up.

A man might tell his fiancée, "After work I'm going to the gym." To which she might reply, "I think I'll meet Kathy for a glass of wine. Why don't you join us when you're done at the gym?"

If he in fact keeps his word, he will indeed go to the gym, not somewhere else. If she keeps her word, assuming Kathy is available, she will actually meet her for a glass of wine. He then will show up, and new plans will develop for the rest of the evening.

These day-to-day agreements prove that we are worthy of our partner's trust. They are little bricks that build and strengthen our relationship. It is these bricks that give our relationship the confidence to grow. As individual points of agreement accumulate, the perceived trustworthiness of our partner grows, and our willingness to trust him or her even more also grows.

It is a good question: "Can two walk together unless they are agreed?" But this same verse reads differently in the Septuagint text of the *Orthodox Study Bible*: "If two people walk together, will each one not come to know the other?" (Amos 3:3, OSB). It is in the journey together that two people come to know each other. Obviously we will learn whether she drinks coffee or not, and whether he drinks his black or with sugar and cream.

But if we take the two translations together, we get a much fuller picture of what it is to walk together. In a world in which marriages are not arranged, and we are pretty much on our own to find a marriage partner, our relationships begin in the dating mode. It is by beginning to do some things together, beginning the walk, that we discover things about each other. We may know after only one date this is not the one I want to walk with through life. Or we may find each other interesting, and so we continue seeing each other. The *Orthodox Study Bible* version is at work while we are dating.

But while we are dating, the King James Version looms on the horizon in the question of marriage. Can two walk down the aisle of marriage if they are not agreed? Dating is a time of getting to know each other. But what we are really getting to know are our shared points of agreement. And the shared points of agreement that count are those that tell us whether we can trust the other person or not.

Can two walk together without getting to know each other? Of course not. But having gotten to know each other, can two continue walking together down a marriage aisle unless they are in agreement? If we have learned that when push comes to shove, when the chips are down, we can't really trust the other person to be there, then we have learned that we are not agreed.

Obviously no one is perfect. Unintentional mistakes do occur. Unforeseen circumstances happen. Events intervene that cause us to be late, forget, or miss what we've agreed to do.

On his way to the gym, your fiancé could have a flat and never make it to the gym. But he could make it in time to join you afterwards, as planned. However, a flat tire is entirely different from his getting a phone call from his friend Blake inviting him to meet him at a sports bar to watch a March Madness basketball game. He agrees, meets Blake, gets caught up in the game, loses track of time, and forgets all about meeting you for a glass of wine. He did not intentionally stand you up, but he also did not guard his point of agreement with you. Was this due to accidental carelessness? Or is he fundamentally careless with relationships? Or is he just careless about his relationship with you? Just as easily as trust can grow, it can be broken.

The impact of a broken point of agreement often depends on how early in a relationship it occurs. Being stood up on a first or second date can be devastating. In *Last Chance Harvey,* Harvey Shine (played by Dustin Hoffman) fails to meet new acquaintance Kate Walker (played by Emma Thompson) because he has a medical episode brought on by having failed to take his prescriptions.

Script writers create such obstacles in order to have a crisis to solve. In real life, broken points of agreement are not so easily fixed. In the Hollywood version, truth and honesty eventually carry the day. Truth and honesty do go hand in hand with being trusted. But in real life our behavior trumps our words. Ultimately it is our behavior, and not our words, that reveals the truth about us.

We cannot live in doubt. We cannot live always wondering if our partner is in fact going where they said they would be going and doing what they said they would be doing.

This point is made in an interesting way in the movie *He's Just Not That Into You.* Janine and Ben (played by Jennifer Connelly and Bradley Cooper) are the only married couple in the movie. Ben eventually cheats on his wife with Anna (played by Scarlett Johansson). When Ben confesses his infidelity, Janine is able to forgive him.

But a continuing theme in their marriage has been the issue of whether Ben is still smoking or not. Multiple times, when confronted by Janine, Ben swears he is no longer smoking. However, after forgiving him for his infidelity, Janine finds a carton of cigarettes hidden among Ben's clothes. It is at this point she kicks him out. The issue was not whether Ben could remain faithful. Ben could no longer be trusted. If he would lie about having stopped smoking, he was capable of lying about having stopped being unfaithful.

When trust is broken, it can only be repaired with truth and honesty. Things must be talked out. Answers must be sought in order for points of agreement once more to be reached. But remember—behavior trumps words. Trust must be earned. And it is earned by our behavior—one event at a time.

No one is perfect. No one. Missed appointments and broken agreements may happen. But it is always easier to keep trust than it is to get it back. This brings us to the fourth cornerstone of our foundation.

FOURTH COSTLY STONE: FORGIVENESS

We've all heard the adage, "To err is human; to forgive is divine." Jonathon Edwards' wrathful and angry view of God notwithstanding,[11] the view that God is a loving and forgiving God is correct. We are most like God when we forgive.

In the Lord's Prayer, Jesus Christ ties the forgiveness of God to our forgiveness of others: in the same manner in which we forgive others, we ask God likewise to forgive us (Matthew 6:9–13; Luke 11:2–4). Christ tells us that the basic human behavior required of us is forgiving others for their mistakes toward us. "For if you forgive men their trespasses, your heavenly Father will also forgive you. But if you do not forgive men their trespasses,

---

11   One of the most famous sermons ever preached in American history was Jonathon Edwards' "Sinners in the Hands of an Angry God," preached July 8, 1741, in Enfield, Connecticut.

neither will your Father forgive your trespasses" (Matthew 6:14–15). Forgiving another person is one of the most readily practicable divine attributes. Every one of us can choose to forgive.

If daily individual points of agreement are little bricks that build and strengthen our relationship, then forgiveness is the cement and mortar that holds the bricks in place and turns individual bricks into a solid relationship.

There will be mistakes in words said, in money spent, in things forgotten, and there will be sins fallen into, and deeds that violate our wedding vows. Birthdays will be forgotten. Anniversaries will not be remembered. Promises will not be kept. Our partner will let us down. We will be disappointed in our partner when, in an unguarded moment, we catch them in the act of being themselves. Life is a process. Each of us is a work in progress. In the same way learning to play the piano takes time and a lot of practice, so too does life. It takes a while to be successful in achieving those daily individual points of agreement. It takes forgiveness to make the process work.

In one of her books, Edith Schaeffer says, "If you demand perfection or nothing, you will always get nothing." None of us is perfect. Neither you nor your partner is perfect. Nor are you today the person you will have become twenty-five years from now. Forgiveness is the way we heal human failure, and with that healing, create the possibility for human growth.

Failures within our relationship cannot be ignored. We must discuss these matters with our partner. When it becomes obvious that we have failed, it is important to humble ourselves and ask for forgiveness. Remember these twelve words:

- ∞ I love you.
- ∞ I am sorry.
- ∞ I will not do it again.

It is easy to become defensive when caught in a mistake. No one sets out to fail. No one likes getting caught in a failure. We are embarrassed to admit our mistake. Our pride gets in the way, and we find it difficult to say, "I'm sorry. I made a mistake." Remember that "by pride comes nothing but strife" (Proverbs 13:10). It takes humility to admit that we were wrong.

Forgiveness must be given freely. It cannot be given with strings attached. Peter asked Christ how many times he had to forgive his brother—perhaps seven times? Christ replied with a number representing infinity—seventy times seven (Matthew 18:21–22). Some people are slow learners, and it will take much forgiveness before those little points of agreement that create trust begin to accumulate.

Forgiven implies forgotten. A failure is not really forgiven if our partner periodically reminds of us it. One groom, in order to have a clean slate with his bride, confessed to her some failures prior to meeting her. During the first year of their marriage, the bride threw up his past failure to him. He replied, "If you want to live in the past, that's your choice. I have been forgiven, and I choose to live in the present." That couple recently celebrated their twenty-fifth wedding anniversary.

Let me add a note of caution. Confessing your failures to your priest or clergy is one thing. But blindsiding your partner or spouse with a confession can lead to explosive consequences. In the movie *He's Just Not That Into You*, with no context and totally out of the blue, while walking down an aisle in a grocery store, Ben blurts out to his wife, Janine, that he has been cheating on her. In the movie *The Wedding Date*, the bride confesses to the groom just prior to the wedding ceremony that she had an affair with the groom's best man while the best man was engaged to the bride's sister. Only in the movies can characters get away with such bombshells. In real life people can end up in a hospital, in jail, on the nightly news, or in the morgue.

It is okay to be angry when hurt by your partner's failure. But be careful that your anger doesn't add fuel to the fire. There is much wisdom in the words, "Be angry but do not sin" (Ephesians 4:26). St. Paul goes on to say, "Do not let the sun go down on your anger." A young groom had been married less than a month when the first disagreement with his wife happened. At eleven o'clock at night he knocked on his parents' door and asked to come in. After he told them he needed to spend the night there, his parents told him he now had a wife and his own home, and his bed was in that home. And with that they sent him home. The son listened to the wisdom of his parents, went home to his wife, and worked out the problem.

Thirty-five years and three children later, that groom walked into their living room and found his wife dead in her recliner. She had died from a heart attack while he was in the back yard. He called me and told me the awful news and asked me to go tell his by-now-elderly parents personally. I drove his parents to their son's home. Thirty-five years earlier, that young groom had listened to the wisdom of his parents and had not let the sun go down on his anger. And thirty-five years later, it was death, not anger, that finally parted them.

We should also remember that people don't think very well when they are tired and exhausted. We may say things when we are tired and irritable that we would never say when we are fresh and relaxed. Getting a good night's sleep often helps us calm down and think more clearly.

Issues will happen. Failures will occur. But with the humility to say "I'm sorry," and the grace to forgive, you can overcome crises in your relationship and in your marriage.

Forgiveness is a two-way street. Both of you must be committed to each other. Our mistakes and failures can bring great pain and hurt to this one we love so much. We must love the other so much that we can swallow our pride and say, "I'm sorry." And we must love the other so much that in spite of the hurt, we will still be able to forgive.

In the movie *Four Christmases*, Brad (Vince Vaughn) and Kate (Reese Witherspoon) have had a disagreement in their response to their in-laws. In the next scene they are driving silently in their car. Kate says, "I don't want to fight anymore." Brad replies, "I don't want to fight either." Marriages do not survive because one of us is right. They survive because both of us can say, "You're more important to me than being right."

One couple had been married less than a year when a disagreement arose. "You can sleep on the couch tonight!" the new bride told her husband. The new husband gently replied, "This is *our* bed. And I'm going to sleep in *our* bed. Now you can sleep in our bed with me if you want; that's your choice. But I'm sleeping in *our* bed."

Nothing had been resolved, but the new bride got in the bed. As the Dixie Chicks sing it, she "wasn't ready to make nice yet." But they at least agreed to sleep in the same bed that night. They kept their backs to each other and remained at least six to twelve inches apart. It was the longest night of their lives. It felt as if they were sleeping on opposite sides of the Grand Canyon. But when they awoke, the anger had passed, and they could begin gently to talk.

A year later the same couple hit another rough spot. The bride knew what her husband would say if she told him he could sleep on the couch. So without saying anything, she took her pillow and some blankets and went to the couch herself. The husband went to sleep in *their* bed. In the middle of the night he got out of bed, went to where his wife was sleeping, and slipped in beside her on the couch. When she realized he was beside her, she said, "Come on, let's go to bed." They got up from the couch and went to sleep together in *their* bed. By their behavior, both finally said, "You're more important to me than being right."

The Courtship of Inanna and Dumuzi is one of the oldest stories in human history; it has existed in written form since 2000 B.C. This ancient romantic story contains these lines:

> He put his hand in her hand.
> He put his hand to her heart.
> Sweet is the sleep of hand to hand.
> Sweeter still the sleep of heart to heart.[12]

Forgiveness begins when we set aside our anger and our pride. It begins when our heart says, "You're more important to me than being right." Forgiveness happens heart to heart.

The four cornerstones of love, faith, trust, and forgiveness will help you build a strong foundation that will support and sustain your relationship as it grows through the years. It was the foolish man who built his house upon the sand, and when the winds and the floods came, the house could not stand. But the wise man built his house upon a rock, and when the winds and the floods came, his house withstood the storms. With God as the center of your home, and with love, faith, trust, and forgiveness as its four cornerstones, you and your spouse can build your life, your relationship, and your home on a strong foundation that will withstand the storms of life.

---

12 "The Courtship of Inanna and Dumuzi" in Diane Wolkstein and Samuel Kramer, *Inanna: Queen of Heaven and Earth* (New York: Harper & Rowe, Publishers, 1983), 43.

CRAYONS AND COLORING BOOKS

One of the skills children master is how to color in a coloring book. All children seem to follow a predictable pattern. At first they use one crayon only, and they color by going back and forth across the picture. There is no intention of staying within the lines. Since they are just now mastering the mechanical skill of holding a crayon, they often press the crayon quite hard upon the paper while rapidly moving their hand across the page.

In the second stage, with better fine motor skill and improved eye-hand coordination, the child progresses to the level of attempting to stay within the lines. One of the first marks that a child has reached stage two is their learning how to use a crayon to outline the area to be colored. By coloring the outline first, the child creates a boundary that defines the area in which a color is to be used.

Initially a child at stage two still thinks monochromatically; they still use only one color. They will use their favorite color almost exclusively. Later they begin alternating colors from picture to picture, but any given picture is still all one color.

Having learned to think in terms of staying within the lines and having discovered a crayon box full of colors, a child next advances to stage three: thinking in multiple colors. The child still makes use of the skills learned from the first two stages. The boy's jeans are outlined in blue, but his shirt is outlined in green. The girl's dress is yellow, but her sash is purple. The child still takes great care to stay within the lines of each color.

A child just beginning to color is not expected to be at stage three. But neither is a child expected to remain at stage one. We expect them to progress developmentally by mastering one stage and moving on to the next.

Just like coloring, a successful marriage begins with learning how to stay inside the lines. When we first began dating, we had not yet learned the social graces. We were a long way from having panache and savoir-faire. We might have been vaguely aware that relationships have boundaries, but we didn't stay within the lines. We told our friends all the details of each date. Did you hold hands? Did he put his arm around you? Did you kiss? And the details got more detailed.

But relationships have boundaries. To become a level three artist, we must learn to stay inside the lines. For a marriage to succeed, it too must stay within the lines. First of all, a marriage must have privacy. What goes on in your marriage should stay within your marriage. Obviously I am not speaking about spiritual issues that you should discuss with your priest. Nor am I speaking about physical, psychological, or sexual abuse. Such issues as these have already crossed the boundary of a marriage, and if you are experiencing them you need to get help from a qualified counselor.

When I say that what goes on in your marriage should stay within your marriage, I am not speaking of such extreme things. I am speaking of the everyday events and behaviors of your relationship. You must have the freedom to relax and be yourselves in front of each other. Your partner will catch you in the act of being yourself many times, and vice versa. But such events must not become gossip outside of your marriage.

In the Orthodox Church, we pray the Communion Prayer before receiving the Eucharist. In this prayer we say, "I will not speak of Thy Mystery to Thine enemies, neither will I give Thee a kiss like Judas." In the same way that our private spiritual life is not to be casually paraded in front of the general public, our private marital life is not something to put on display. We must be careful to guard our spouse and to guard our marriage. Our spouse must be able to trust us in order to entrust himself or herself to us. We cannot give them a kiss in the bedroom and then betray the secrets of our marriage to the guys or gals at work.

Below are some lines to stay within in living our marriages. It is tempting to call them "The Ten Commandments of Marriage" or "The Rules of Marriage." But we in the Orthodox Church understand the canons of the Church, the canon law if you will, not in the rigid, legally binding sense of Western law; we understand them in a helpful, useful way, as guidelines for how we are to do things. The goal of the church canons is not cold, legal obedience, but a warm, living agreement of becoming one in practice. Therefore I have chosen to call these "guidelines." They are lines that guide us, and lines that we will benefit by staying within as we live our marriage.[13]

GUIDELINES OF MARRIAGE FOR WIVES

- Live within your means, or preferably, a little under your means.
- Do not demean your husband in front of others.
- Do not deceive your husband or hide or keep anything from him.
- Assist your husband in good things, but do not condone any wrongdoing on his part.
- Do not mock, humiliate, or embarrass your husband by your speech, dress, or behavior.
- Do not flirt with other men. Be a lady. Remember your vows.
- If things go wrong, do not throw the day away. Try to remain positive and make the best of the situation. Become part of the solution, not part of the problem.
- Always remember in marriage, two become one. Your unity is essential.
- Always place God first in the center of your life, before yourself or your husband.
- Be careful not to complain or nag constantly.

GUIDELINES OF MARRIAGE FOR HUSBANDS

- Do not act or live as a dictator. Be considerate and reasonable.
- Do not look for faults or mistakes, always trying to find something wrong.
- Do not be selfish, greedy, or claim everything as yours. It is not *your* house or *your* children. It is *our* house and *our* children.

---

13 The following guidelines are adapted from various articles by C. M. Ward that appeared in *Pulpit Helps,* April 1983, and other articles that appeared in *Family Helps,* edited by Dr. Spiros Zodhiates, Vol. 4 No. 2 (1983).

- Do not initiate arguments or start battles. Be at peace with your wife.

- Do not speak against or criticize your wife in front of others, nor reveal her faults publicly. Rather speak lovingly and privately with her.

- Do not take your marriage for granted. Continue falling in love with your wife and continue courting her, dating her, and winning her.

- Do not always demand your way. Marriage is "give and take." In the Orthodox wedding you have crowned each other as king and queen. You share the throne together.

- Do not shrink or run away from taking responsibility as a husband. Face your obligation with conviction.

- Do not waste your time, but spend quality time with your wife. Invest in your wife by communicating with her, being creative with her, and encouraging her.

- Show or express your appreciation for your wife in words and deeds. Do not be conceited. Be kind, thoughtful, and considerate. Remember, she is your best friend.

Now you know why I call them guidelines! Just like learning to use crayons and a coloring book, it will take a lot of practice, a lot of trial and error, and a lot of forgiveness to learn how to stay within the guidelines of your marriage. Happy coloring!

CAMELOT IT'S NOT

The title song of the musical *Camelot* contains the lines:

> In short there's simply not
> a more congenial spot
> for happily-ever-aftering
> than here in Camelot.[14]

Fairy tales (and romantic movies) begin with "Once upon a time" and end with living "happily ever after." In between we have (1) boy meets girl, (2) boy falls in love with girl, (3) boy loses girl, and (4) boy wins girl. Change the names, change the location, and change the crisis—it is still the same story. But what happens the day after "happily ever after"?

Marriages begin where the fairy tales end. The wedding is over. Think of it—this thing that has consumed all your attention for months is over! The whirlwind events of the week before your wedding, the wedding itself, your reception, and leaving for your honeymoon are one seamless blur.

Now you are in your new home. Your marriage has begun. There are hundreds of decisions to make. Which picture goes where? Where does the television go? How do we arrange the furniture? Which drawer does the silverware go in? Which grocery store shall we use? What's our budget? Do you eat breakfast?

From this day forward, you and your spouse will be making countless and endless joint decisions. Decisions require give and take, negotiation,

---

14 Alan Jay Lerner, "Camelot," title song from the 1960 Broadway musical.

and surrender. Married life is about daily adapting to the needs and issues each day brings. You will need to adapt daily to each other's physical, emotional, spiritual, and financial needs.

When you were single, you were independent. For the most part, your decisions were your own. You only had yourself to please.

But now you are not single. You are not alone. Two are becoming one. You are now dependent on each other. You cannot act independently of each other.

Perhaps you remember as a child competing in a three-legged race. In a three-legged race everyone is teamed with a partner. You stand side by side and tie your left leg to the other's right leg. When the two of you run, you must figure out how to run in harmony—both outside legs moving forward together and then the tied right and left leg moving forward together. The two fastest runners, once tied together, often come in last. It is the team that can be in harmony and simultaneously move the correct legs that will win the race.

One of the greatest difficulties faced by engaged couples is the transition from dating life to married life. Dating is a matter of individuals meeting and getting to know each other. Dating is a two-legged activity in which we select our partner for the three-legged activity of marriage.

Dating is partly fantasy—the romance and thrill of being introduced to a larger world of new people and new experiences. But marriage is not dating. Yes, there is still romance in marriage. But marriage is life being lived realistically. In the real world that most of us will live in, we do not eat out at fancy restaurants every night. We don't fly across the globe every weekend to exotic locales as if we were contestants on the television show *The Bachelor*.

Marriage is about creating a home, our home, a home that will protect the two of us emotionally from the storms of life, that will nurture us and allow our marriage to flourish, and that one day, God willing, we will fill with children and give them life.

The transition from the single life to married life is huge. This transition is CHANGE with all capital letters:

- CHANGE in your lifestyle
- CHANGE in where you live

- ✑ CHANGE in your friends
- ✑ CHANGE in your family
- ✑ CHANGE in your attitudes
- ✑ CHANGE in your finances

When you say "I do," the transition is immediate. You don't get to keep one foot in the single world and one foot in the married world.

But other kinds of change come gradually. Some changes come our way without our recognizing them. Some are in ourselves, in the way we do things or accomplish things. These changes come to us as differences:

- ✑ DIFFERENCE in our opinions
- ✑ DIFFERENCE in our expectations
- ✑ DIFFERENCE in our appearance
- ✑ DIFFERENCE in our personality
- ✑ DIFFERENCE in our physical body

Remember, the fairy tale is over. Your marriage begins when the fairy tale ends.

- ✑ You may think a good marriage will always be romantic. This is a myth. The fairy tale is over.
- ✑ You may think of marriage as always being filled with happiness. This is a myth. The fairy tale is over.
- ✑ You may think as long as you love each other, everything else will always just fall into place. This is a myth. The fairy tale is over.
- ✑ You may think your spouse has only one goal in your marriage—to meet your needs. This is a myth. The fairy tale is over.
- ✑ You may think that having a disagreement or conflict in your marriage means your spouse doesn't love you. This is a myth. The fairy tale is over.

Marriage is lived in the real world with real people. It requires adapting to the changing circumstances of life. This change requires, first and foremost, talking to each other. Communication is absolutely necessary.

There will be crises. There will be doubts, and there will be fear. Satan is always laboring to bring conflict and defeat into our lives. Maintain your communication. Keep your trust and intimacy for each other to see you through the crises and to rebuild and repair any damage that has been done to your marriage.

Marriage is not a fairy tale. Do not panic, thinking your world is over. It is over when you neglect the intervention of God, the Church, and qualified counselors. Your marriage needs constant nurturing. Your relationship will always be in a state of flux. It is a dynamic partnership, not a static contract.

Marriage requires being sensitive to one another's needs and adapting to each other for the rest of your lives. The person you are today is not the person you will be tomorrow. You are in the transition from being single and running a two-legged race to being married and running a three-legged race. You will be changing and adapting to each other for the rest of your lives.

It is impossible to say it often enough—communication is the key. It has been estimated that forty percent of our communication with our spouse involves acts or words of intimacy, twenty percent is body language and nonverbal communication, twenty percent is verbal communication, and twenty percent is the interaction of our bodies with each other while we sleep.

We must learn how to listen to each other. We must really hear what our spouse is saying. We have to learn how to do this. We have to be patient with each other and teach the other person how to listen to us. We need to stop, gently get their attention, and say to them, "Can we sit and talk? This is really important, and I need to tell you what I'm feeling."

Sometimes we need to tell our spouse, "I don't expect you to fix this. I don't expect you to do anything about my problem. I just need to talk about what's going on with me at work (or with my parents, or with the kids)."

Talking is all about getting to know the heart of our spouse. We need to know when our spouse is wounded. Sometimes we are the cause, and we can say, "I'm sorry," and begin working on ways to heal the wound. Sometimes we are not the cause, and there is nothing we can do to fix the situation. But there is healing in opening our hearts to the pain in our spouse's heart. There is healing in sharing another's pain, even when there is nothing we can do to remove the pain.

Remember—in the fairy tale, everyone is perfect and knows how to talk and listen perfectly. But the marriage begins when the fairy tale ends. In a marriage we do not know how to say what we feel. And we do not know how to listen. If I want my wife to listen to my heart, I must patiently and gently teach her how to listen to me. No one is very good at the three-legged race in the beginning. But with laughter, forgiveness, patience, and gentleness we can learn how to be experts at three-legged racing. I can learn how to listen to my wife, and she can learn how to listen to me.

Remember the words of the ancient story quoted earlier:

> He put his hand in her hand.
> He put his hand to her heart.
> Sweet is the sleep of hand-to-hand.
> Sweeter still the sleep of heart-to-heart.

There is good reason a private and intimate conversation is known as a "heart-to-heart" talk. Next to your relationship with God, your marriage is the most important relationship in your lives. The investment you make in each other, in learning how to share your heart with each other and in learning how to listen to each other, will pay off. There is nothing sweeter than having achieved a heart-to-heart marriage.

Through the years I have collected many little pieces of advice and encouragement for newlyweds and long-time-marrieds as well. If you want your marriage to become a heart-to-heart marriage, you should find this useful.

HINTS FOR A HEART-TO-HEART MARRIAGE

1. Never both be angry at the same time.
2. Never yell at each other unless the house is on fire.
3. Yield to the wishes of the other as an exercise in self-discipline, if you can't think of a better reason.
4. If you have a choice between making yourself look good and making your mate look good, choose your mate.
5. If you have any criticism, make it lovingly.
6. Never, ever bring up a mistake of the past.

7.   Neglect the whole world rather than each other.
8.   Never let the day end without saying at least one kind or complimentary thing to your mate.
9.   Never meet without an affectionate welcome.
10. Never let the sun go down on an argument unresolved.
11. When you do wrong, make sure you have talked it out and have asked for forgiveness.
12. Remember it takes two to quarrel. The one with the least sense is the one who will be doing the most talking.
                                        —Author Unknown

Stress is another great enemy of a healthy marriage. Many external threats and issues can bring stress on our marriage. However, let me speak here of the personal stress we bring home from work. At the very least, work-related stress makes us easily frustrated, short-tempered, and awfully poor listeners. Therefore, if we can find some useful tools that help relieve or reduce our stress before or on first arriving home, it will free us up to be fully present once we are home. We then can be kind, gentle, gracious, and attentive listeners.

If you take the same route home from work every day, you may find it useful to have a particular billboard, tree, or telephone pole on which you consciously "hang" your job stress while going home. It will be waiting for you when you pass by the next morning, and you can "pick it up" then and take it with you back to work. Below are some tools you may find particularly useful in helping you relax and reduce stress.

TOOLS FOR RELAXING

1.   Sprinkle one-minute quiet periods through the busiest part of your day. This will break the strain, keep you effective until the day's end, and make you fresher on returning home.
2.   Get fifteen minutes of continuous quiet at some time during the day.
3.   During this quiet period, use definite relaxation techniques. Physical, mental, and spiritual disciplines can reduce tension.
4.   Inhale and exhale three long breaths. Raise your arms and allow

your hands to fall on your knees like a wet leaf on a log. What is more relaxed than a wet leaf on a log?

5. Conceive of God's relaxing peace as touching, in turn, every muscle in your body, beginning with your toes, moving upward, and finally resting on your eyes.

6. Relax your mind by imagination. Mentally you can take a trip without going anywhere at all. Daydream for a few moments.

7. In your imagination, dwell for a moment on the most peaceful and beautiful scenes you can visualize.

8. By your thought, attach your life to God's re-creative energy. Think of yourself as being renewed physically, emotionally, and spiritually.

9. Insert your name in the blanks of each of the following statements. Every day repeat each statement three times. "You will keep _____ in perfect peace, whose mind is stayed on You." "Come unto Me, _____, and I will give you rest." "Peace I give unto _____."

10. Drain your mind of hate, impure thinking, dishonest desires, and fears. These are the infection centers of tension. When they are drained away, relaxation can become complete.

Fairy tales are delightfully entertaining stories. Dating is fun. But neither fairy tales nor dating is a match for the remarkable joys and happiness of a heart-to-heart marriage. Real marriages begin where the fairy tales leave off.

THE NEWLYWED GAME

The Newlywed Game is one of the most popular television game shows ever produced. Created by Nick Nicholson and Roger Muir and produced by Church Barris, *The Newlywed Game* debuted in 1966. Different versions were created through the years, but the original host, Bob Eubanks, has remained with the show and hosted the Spring 2010 version.

The premise of *The Newlywed Game* is to ask newly married couples a series of questions designed to reveal how well the spouses know each other. The answers are often surprising and reveal more than the contestants expected. Some contestants, competitive and wanting to win, become angry with their spouses and, forgetting to protect them, actually get into heated arguments in front of the audience.

The real lesson to be learned from *The Newlywed Game* is that newly married couples don't know their spouses very well. That this is so always comes as a shock to the newlyweds. They are so certain they know each other well. But here's the real shocker: If those married for less than a year don't know each other very well, then those of us about to get married really don't know our intended spouse. We know them less today than we will after being married a year, and even after a year we still won't really know them well.

I want you to play *The Newlywed Game* with your spouse or fiancé(e). In Round 1, each of you must answer the following questions by yourselves and without any assistance from the other. These are not trick questions, nor do they have a hidden sexual meaning. These are real questions about everyday stuff. Respond to each question by predicting how your spouse or fiancé(e) will answer, and then give your own answer. If you choose "other," explain in the blank provided. After both of you have responded privately and separately to all the questions, go to Round 2.

THE NEWLYWED QUESTIONNAIRE

ROUND 1

HOW WELL DO HUSBANDS KNOW THEIR WIVES?

QUESTIONS FOR THE WOMAN

1. How does your husband or fiancé act when he meets new people?
   a. outgoing
   b. sociable
   c. shy

2. I would like our home to be decorated
   a. Early American
   b. Contemporary
   c. Spanish American
   d. French Provincial
   e. Mediterranean
   f. other _____

3. I honestly feel that communication is one area we
   a. are very good at
   b. are okay with
   c. should work harder on

4. If I had to change one thing about my husband or fiancé's appearance, it would be his
   a. hairstyle
   b. style of dress

c. weight
d. other _____

5. My parents have met my future in-laws.
   a. yes
   b. no

6. My husband/fiancé is more of the
   a. stay-at-home type
   b. always-on-the-go type

7. Sex is one topic we talk little about.
   a. agree
   b. disagree

8. My husband/fiancé readily shares his feelings with me.
   a. always
   b. most of the time
   c. occasionally
   d. never

9. When my husband/fiancé is upset, he gets
   a. angry
   b. violent
   c. silent
   d. withdrawn

10. What would be our greatest monthly expense?
    a. housing
    b. food
    c. car payment
    d. other _____

11. What concerns your husband/fiancé most about your marriage?
    a. commitment

  b. finances

  c. being a parent

  d. finding a place to live

  e. spiritual life

  f. I'm not sure

  g. other _____

12. Who is/will be the "bookkeeper" in your family?

  a. myself

  b. my husband/fiancé

  c. both of us

13. I have some outstanding debts he doesn't know about.

  a. agree

  b. disagree

14. My husband/fiancé intends to pursue a career.

  a. agree

  b. disagree

15. I now have

  a. no credit cards

  b. one credit card

  c. two credit cards

  d. more than two credit cards

16. My spiritual practices include

  a. daily prayers

  b. daily religious readings

  c. participating in Vespers

  d. participating in Divine Liturgy

  e. participating in choir

  f. participating in Sunday school

  g. participating in church organizations

  h. none of the above

17. One thing we seldom discuss is
     a.   faith
     b.   sex
     c.   in-laws
     d.   intimacy
     e.   feelings
     f.   other _____

18. What are/will be our monthly housing and utility costs?
     a.   Under $500
     b. $500–1000
     c. $1000–1500
     d. $1500–2000
     e.   above $2,000

19. I have spent time with my (future) in-laws
     a.   frequently
     b.   occasionally
     c.   one time
     d.   not at all

20. When we disagree, my first reaction is
     a.   argue verbally
     b.   become defensive
     c.   use the "silent treatment"
     d.   give in

21. When spending time with your husband/fiancé, are you
     a.   nervous
     b.   excited
     c.   calm
     d.   uncertain

22. Who will do the cooking?
     a.   husband/fiancé
     b.   yourself
     c.   both

23.   My husband/fiancé attempts to "spare me" from his bad
      moods
      a.   always
      b.   occasionally
      c.   sometimes
      d.   never

24.   Is your husband/fiancé
      a.   strong-willed
      b.   flexible
      c.   stubborn

25.   Who will be the wage earner in your family?
      a.   husband
      b.   wife
      c.   both

26.   My husband/fiancé uses alcohol and/or mind-altering
      substances
      a.   often
      b.   regularly
      c.   rarely
      d.   never

27.   We have made an attempt to make a budget for our family to
      follow.
      a.   yes
      b.   no

28.   Who will be the principal disciplinarian for your children?
      a.   husband
      b.   wife
      c.   both

29.   What form of birth control do/will you use?
      a.   the Pill
      b.   diaphragm

c.   condom
d.   foam
e.   I.U.D.
f.   calendar rhythm
g.   sympto-thermal method
h.   no birth control
i.   I'm not sure
j.   other _____

30. Have you ever seen your husband/fiancé cry?
     a.   yes
     b.   no

31. When we argue, my tactic is
     a.   mentioning his old girlfriend
     b.   bringing up his past mistakes
     c.   not saying anything at all
     d.   other _____
     e.   I never use these tactics

32. I sometimes wonder if my husband/fiancé is/will be satisfied with me sexually.
     a.   agree
     b.   disagree

33. When it comes to spending, who is/will be the most conservative?
     a.   you
     b.   your husband/fiancé
     c.   both

34. How many children would you like to have?
     a.   none
     b.   one
     c.   two
     d.   three
     e.   more than three

35. I would characterize my husband/fiancé as
    a. aggressive
    b. passive

36. We go out on a date
    a. once a week
    b. twice a month
    c. once a month
    d. less than once a month

PREDICTIONS BY THE MAN

Please predict the answer your fiancée/wife gave to each question.

1. How does your husband or fiancé act when he meets new people?
    a. outgoing
    b. sociable
    c. shy

2. I would like our home to be decorated
    a. Early American
    b. Contemporary
    c. Spanish American
    d. French Provincial
    e. Mediterranean
    f. other _____

3. I honestly feel that communication is one area we
    a. are very good at
    b. are okay with
    c. should work harder on

4. If I had to change one thing about my husband or fiancé's appearance, it would be his
    a. hairstyle
    b. style of dress

    c.   weight

    d.   other _____

5.   My parents have met my future in-laws.

    a.   yes

    b.   no

6.   My husband/fiancé is more of the

    a.   stay-at-home type

    b.   always-on-the-go type

7.   Sex is one topic we talk little about.

    a.   agree

    b.   disagree

8.   My husband/fiancé readily shares his feelings with me.

    a.   always

    b.   most of the time

    c.   occasionally

    d.   never

9.   When my husband/fiancé is upset, he gets

    a.   angry

    b.   violent

    c.   silent

    d.   withdrawn

10.   What would be our greatest monthly expense?

    a.   housing

    b.   food

    c.   car payment

    d.   other _____

11.   What concerns your husband/fiancé most about your marriage?

    a.   commitment

    b.   finances

      c.   being a parent

      d.   finding a place to live

      e.   spiritual life

      f.   I'm not sure

      g.   other _____

12. Who is/will be the "bookkeeper" in your family?
   a. myself
   b. my husband/fiancé
   c. both of us

13. I have some outstanding debts he doesn't know about.
   a. agree
   b. disagree

14. My husband/fiancé intends to pursue a career.
   a. agree
   b. disagree

15. I now have
   a. no credit cards
   b. one credit card
   c. two credit cards
   d. more than two credit cards

16. My spiritual practices include
   a. daily prayers
   b. daily religious readings
   c. participating in Vespers
   d. participating in Divine Liturgy
   e. participating in choir
   f. participating in Sunday school
   g. participating in church organizations
   h. none of the above

17. One thing we seldom discuss is
   a. faith

b.   sex
c.   in-laws
d.   intimacy
e.   feelings
f.   other _____

18.   What are/will be our monthly housing and utility costs?
   a.   Under $500
   b. $500–1000
   c. $1000–1500
   d. $1500–2000
   e.   above $2,000

19.   I have spent time with my (future) in-laws
   a.   frequently
   b.   occasionally
   c.   one time
   d.   not at all

20.   When we disagree, my first reaction is
   a.   argue verbally
   b.   become defensive
   c.   use the "silent treatment"
   d.   give in

21.   When spending time with your husband/fiancé, are you
   e.   nervous
   f.   excited
   g.   calm
   h.   uncertain

22.   Who will do the cooking?
   a.   husband/fiancé
   b.   yourself
   c.   both

23. My husband/fiancé attempts to "spare me" from his bad
    moods
    a.   always
    b.   occasionally
    c.   sometimes
    d.   never

24. Is your husband/fiancé
    a.   strong-willed
    b.   flexible
    c.   stubborn

25. Who will be the wage earner in your family?
    a.   husband
    b.   wife
    c.   both

26. My husband/fiancé uses alcohol and/or mind-altering
    substances
    a.   often
    b.   regularly
    c.   rarely
    d.   Never

27. We have made an attempt to make a budget for our family to
    follow.
    a.   yes
    b.   no

28. Who will be the principal disciplinarian for your children?
    a.   husband
    b.   wife
    c.   both

29. What form of birth control do/will you use?
    a.   the Pill
    b.   diaphragm

    c.   condom
    d.   foam
    e.   I.U.D.
    f.   calendar rhythm
    g.   sympto-thermal method
    h.   no birth control
    i.   I'm not sure
    j.   other _____

30. Have you ever seen your husband/fiancé cry?
    a.   yes
    b.   no

31. When we argue, my tactic is
    a.   mentioning his old girlfriend
    b.   bringing up his past mistakes
    c.   not saying anything at all
    d.   other _____
    e.   I never use these tactics

32. I sometimes wonder if my husband/fiancé is/will be satisfied with me sexually.
    a.   agree
    b.   disagree

33. When it comes to spending, who is/will be the most conservative?
    a.   you
    b.   your husband/fiancé
    c.   both

34. How many children would you like to have?
    a.   none
    b.   one
    c.   two
    d.   three
    e.   more than three

35. I would characterize my husband/fiancé as
    a. aggressive
    b. passive

36. We go out on a date
    a. once a week
    b. twice a month
    c. once a month
    d. less than once a month

ROUND 2

HOW WELL DO WIVES KNOW THEIR HUSBANDS?

QUESTIONS FOR THE MAN

1. My wife/fiancée's parents are enthused about our marriage.
   a. agree
   b. disagree

2. My wife/fiancée
   a. is easily discouraged
   b. is fearful of the unknown
   c. never will discuss death

3. Arguing is a bad thing.
   a. agree
   b. disagree

4. When will you start a family?
   a. right away
   b. in a year or two
   c. when we have both finished our education
   d. I'm not sure
   e. other _____

5. I solved/will solve some problems by getting married.
    a. agree
    b. disagree

6. Number the following in your order of preference with 1 as the most favored.
    _____ going to sporting events
    _____ going to a concert
    _____ going to a movie
    _____ staying at home and watching TV
    _____ going to a bar
    _____ being with friends

7. How does your wife/fiancée handle an argument?
    a. listens and talks
    b. ignores and forgets
    c. gets defensive or leaves
    d. silence

8. There are times when it is difficult to get my wife/fiancée's attention.
    a. agree
    b. disagree

9. I would most like to live
    a. in a big city
    b. in a small town
    c. in a suburb
    d. in the country

10. How many couples do you have for friends?
    a. none
    b. one
    c. two
    d. three or more

11.   Which would you rather do?
    a.   go camping for the weekend
    b.   visit relatives for the weekend
    c.   visit a city you have never been to before for a weekend
    d.   spend the weekend at a nice local hotel

12.   I attend Divine Liturgy
    a.   regularly
    b.   on special days
    c.   rarely

13.   How much time do you spend talking together?
    a.   a lot
    b.   a moderate amount
    c.   some
    d.   very little

14.   My wife/fiancée and I have a hobby that we share.
    a.   agree
    b.   disagree

15.   If my wife/fiancée has a difficult decision to make, she
    a.   consults with me always
    b.   consults with me occasionally
    c.   works it through on her own

16.   My wife/fiancée is a
    a.   better listener than talker
    b.   better talker than listener

17.   I intend to pursue a career.
    a.   agree
    b.   disagree

18.   I regard my faith as being of ultimate importance in my life.
    a.   agree
    b.   disagree

19. My wife/fiancée and I are from the same religious background.
    a. agree
    b. disagree

20. What concerns you most about getting married?
    a. becoming tied down
    b. money
    c. being a parent
    d. finding a place to live
    e. I'm not sure

21. We will be living in
    f. a house
    g. an apartment
    h. with relatives
    i. other _____

22. I have seen my wife/fiancée least when she is
    a. discouraged
    b. angry
    c. happy
    d. depressed
    e. other _____

23. I take part in some church activities besides regular services (i.e., choir, study groups, committees, etc.).
    a. agree
    b. disagree

24. I use alcohol and/or other mind-altering substances
    a. often
    b. regularly
    c. rarely
    d. never

25. I would characterize my wife/fiancée as
    a. strong-willed
    b. flexible

26. My wife/fiancée has habits that annoy me.
    a. one
    b. two
    c. several

27. We have looked into getting health and life insurance.
    a. agree
    b. disagree

28. My parents are enthused about our marriage.
    c. agree
    d. disagree

29. With your wife/fiancée, would you rather
    a. go to a party
    b. go to dinner and a movie
    c. stay at home

30. We spend an average of
    a. 2 hours per day together
    b. 4 hours per day together
    c. 6 hours per day together
    d. more than 6 hours per day

31. When I am with my (future) in-laws, I
    a. worry about their impressions of me
    b. feel at home with them
    c. feel insecure about their feelings for me
    d. I seldom see my (future) in-laws

32. Who talks more?
    a. you
    b. wife/fiancée
    c. both

33. My wife/fiancée knows little about my personality and behavior
    a. in the morning
    b. late at night
    c. when I am in a bad mood
    d. when I am sick
    e. more than one of the above

34. The time that we talk the most is
    a. when we are in the car
    b. when we eat together
    c. just sitting around
    d. other _____

35. We will have
    e. a joint checking account
    a. individual accounts
    b. no checking accounts

36. On the topic of sexuality, I feel that I
    a. am well informed
    b. have basic knowledge
    c. would like some more information

37. I know
    a. most of my wife/fiancée's friends
    b. few of her friends
    c. none of her friends

PREDICTIONS BY THE WOMAN
Please predict the answer your fiancé/husband gave.

1. My wife/fiancée's parents are enthused about our marriage.
   a. agree
   b. disagree

2. My wife/fiancée
   a. is easily discouraged
   b. is fearful of the unknown
   c. never will discuss death

3. Arguing is a bad thing.
   a. agree
   b. disagree

4. When will you start a family?
   a. right away
   b. in a year or two
   c. when we have both finished our education
   d. I'm not sure
   e. other _____

5. I solved/will solve some problems by getting married.
   a. agree
   b. disagree

6. Number the following in your order of preference with 1 as the most favored.
   _____ going to sporting events
   _____ going to a concert
   _____ going to a movie
   _____ staying at home and watching TV
   _____ going to a bar
   _____ being with friends

7.   How does your wife/fiancée handle an argument?
   a.   listens and talks
   b.   ignores and forgets
   c.   gets defensive or leaves
   d.   silence

8.   There are times when it is difficult to get my wife/fiancée's attention.
   e.   agree
   f.   disagree

9.   I would most like to live
   a.   in a big city
   b.   in a small town
   c.   in a suburb
   d.   in the country

10.   How many couples do you have for friends?
   a.   none
   b.   one
   c.   two
   d.   three or more

11.   Which would you rather do?
   a.   go camping for the weekend
   b.   visit relatives for the weekend
   c.   visit a city you have never been to before for a weekend
   d.   spend the weekend at a nice local hotel

12.   I attend Divine Liturgy
   a.   regularly
   b.   on special days
   c.   rarely

13.   How much time do you spend talking together?
   a.   a lot
   b.   a moderate amount

    c.   some

    d.   very little

14.   My wife/fiancée and I have a hobby that we share.
   a.   agree
   b.   disagree

15.   If my wife/fiancée has a difficult decision to make, she
   c.   consults with me always
   d.   consults with me occasionally
   e.   works it through on her own

16.   My wife/fiancée is a
   a.   better listener than talker
   b.   better talker than listener

17.   I intend to pursue a career.
   a.   agree
   b.   disagree

18.   I regard my faith as being of ultimate importance in my life.
   a.   agree
   b.   disagree

19.   My wife/fiancée and I are from the same religious background.
   a.   agree
   b.   disagree

20.   What concerns you most about getting married?
   a.   becoming tied down
   b.   money
   c.   being a parent
   d.   finding a place to live
   e.   I'm not sure

21. We will be living in
    a. a house
    b. an apartment
    c. with relatives
    d. other _____

22. I have seen my wife/fiancée least when she is
    a. discouraged
    b. angry
    c. happy
    d. depressed
    e. other _____

23. I take part in some church activities besides regular services (i.e., choir, study groups, committees, etc.).
    a. agree
    b. disagree

24. I use alcohol and/or other mind-altering substances
    a. often
    b. regularly
    c. rarely
    d. never

25. I would characterize my wife/fiancée as
    a. strong-willed
    b. flexible

26. My wife/fiancée has habits that annoy me.
    a. one
    b. two
    c. several

27. We have looked into getting health and life insurance.
    a. agree
    b. disagree

28. My parents are enthused about our marriage.
     a.   agree
     b.   disagree

29. With your wife/fiancée, would you rather
     a.   go to a party
     b.   go to dinner and a movie
     c.   stay at home

30. We spend an average of
     a.   2 hours per day together
     b.   4 hours per day together
     c.   6 hours per day together
     d.   more than 6 hours per day

31. When I am with my (future) in-laws, I
     a.   worry about their impressions of me
     b.   feel at home with them
     c.   feel insecure about their feelings for me
     d.   I seldom see my (future) in-laws

32. Who talks more?
     a.   you
     b.   wife/fiancée
     c.   both

33. My wife/fiancée knows little about my personality and behavior
     a.   in the morning
     b.   late at night
     c.   when I am in a bad mood
     d.   when I am sick
     e.   more than one of the above

34. The time that we talk the most is
     a.   when we are in the car

      b.   when we eat together
      c.   just sitting around
      d.   other _____

35.   We will have
      a.   a joint checking account
      b.   individual accounts
      c.   no checking accounts

36.   On the topic of sexuality, I feel that I
      a.   am well informed
      b.   have basic knowledge
      c.   would like some more information

37.   I know
      a.   most of my wife/fiancée's friends
      b.   few of her friends
      c.   none of her friends

This ends Round 2. Please skim through your completed survey to see that you haven't neglected to answer any of the questions. Remember that your openness and completeness will make this inventory the most helpful.

Now answer the questions for Round 3. In this round you will only answer for yourself.

ROUND 3

THE IN-LAW INVENTORY

Place a check next to each statement that applies to you. If you are not yet married, answer the questions in terms of your future in-laws. Remember, you are answering these questions only for yourself.

1.   In relating to my in-laws I:
     _____ feel very comfortable in knowing what to call them
     _____ wish I knew what to call them (Mom, Dad, or first
             name)

2.   I feel that my spouse is:
     _____ too close to his/her family
     _____ not close enough to his/her family

3.   My spouse feels that I am:
     _____ too close to my family
     _____ not close enough to my family

4.   I wish:
     _____ I felt more comfortable with my spouse's family
     _____ my spouse felt more comfortable with my family

5.   My spouse and I disagree over:
     _____ how much time to spend with family
     _____ whose family to visit for the holidays

6.   I sometimes feel pulled between:
     _____ what my family wants from me and what my spouse
             wants from me
     _____ my loyalty to my own family and my loyalty to my
             spouse's family

7.   Since our wedding, my relationship with my own family:
     _____ has changed for the better
     _____ has changed for the worse

8.   Since our wedding, my relationship with my spouse's family:
     _____ has changed for the better
     _____ has changed for the worse

ROUND 4

REVEALING YOUR ANSWERS

Now that you have answered all the questions, it is time to share your answers with each other. Get comfortable. Turn off your cell phones. Put on a pot of coffee or make some hot chocolate, or fix a cheese tray and pour a glass of wine—whatever the two of you enjoy doing when you are relaxing and talking together.

Begin with Round 1. The fiancée/wife should share her answer to the first question, and the fiancé/husband should reveal what he predicted her answer would be. Move through all the questions, then take a break. Freshen the drinks. When you return for Round 2, the fiancé/husband will share his answer to the first question, to which the fiancée/wife in turn reveals her prediction. Again proceed through all the questions. Take another break before beginning to share your answers to Round 3. Take turns talking about each of your answers.

By the time you have finished, you will discover that neither of you knows the other as well as you thought you did. When you have finished, you will also be astonished at how much better you know your fiancé/ spouse than you did to begin with. And that's the real purpose and the real fun of playing *The Newlywed Game*—to discover who our fiancé/spouse really is. So relax and enjoy getting to know each other on a brand new level.

CONCLUSION

In every way imaginable throughout the pages of Part I, there has been a constant message—for a marriage to work, it takes work. The number one tool used in the work of marriage is communication. Marriage is a relationship. Whatever else a marriage relationship may be, it always includes and is based on communication.

A husband and wife must talk with each other. You must learn to ask your spouse questions. In addition to the specific content of an answer, your spouse is always revealing who they are. To learn how to hear who someone is (which is often hidden behind the words they are saying) takes a lifetime. The first step is learning to talk with each other. The second step is learning how to listen to your spouse's heart. It takes a lifetime to discover who your partner is. It takes a lifetime to discover who you are with your partner.

A lifetime is a long time. That's why marriages are meant for the long haul. Marriages require a "till death do we part" attitude. New couples mark the fact they have been dating by celebrating their first-month anniversary together. Married couples count by years and particularly mark the milestones of the twenty-fifth, the fiftieth, and the seventy-fifth wedding anniversaries.

Invest yourself in your spouse. Invest yourself in your marriage. At the end of the day, whether it's been a thousand, ten thousand, or ten thousand more days, your marriage will have sustained your love for each other, and you will know that next to your relationship with God, your spouse is the best thing that ever happened to you.

"Therefore a man shall leave his father and mother and be joined to his wife, and they shall become one flesh." (Genesis 2:24)

PART II

ORTHODOX
WEDDING

The

Chapter 11

PRE-WEDDING INSTRUCTIONS

Your wedding is an historic event that you will remember for the rest of your life. For the Orthodox believer, in order for this day to be as special and wonderful as it can be, the guidelines of the Church must be followed. Before discussing the marriage rite itself, let us first turn our attention to the basic instructions that govern an Orthodox wedding.[15]

MARRIAGE IN THE ORTHODOX CHURCH IS A SACRAMENT

The Sacrament of Holy Matrimony is one of the Holy Mysteries of the Orthodox Church. It unites a man and a woman both spiritually and physically into one cohesive unit that respects and proclaims each one's individual personality while mystically drawing together the man, the woman, and the Holy Spirit into one family.

As a sacrament, the ceremony acknowledges the Presence of the Almighty God in the service. What may or may not be done in the wedding ceremony is set by the Church. You are asking to receive the Church's Sacrament of Marriage; you are not renting the church as a setting for your own wedding. You may not create your own service or modify the Church's Sacrament of Marriage. Because the Church is the Body of Christ, we do not sponsor "designer weddings."

---

15 I am grateful to Fr. John Salem for sharing with me his ideas and specific examples for briefing couples preparing for an Orthodox wedding, some of which are incorporated in the discussion that follows.

CONFIRM YOUR WEDDING DATE WITH YOUR PRIEST

A reservation for the Sacrament of Marriage is not definite until you have met with the pastor at least three months prior to the wedding (six months to a year is preferred) and confirmed a date. Please be aware and respectful that there are seasons and days when marriages do not take place in the Orthodox Church.

Prohibited Days:
- Every Wednesday and Friday throughout the year (days of fasting)
- The eve of every Sunday (i.e., after sunset on Saturdays)
- September 14 (The Elevation of the Cross)
- December 24–25 (Christmas)
- January 5–6 (Epiphany)
- February 1–2 (The Presentation of Christ in the Temple)
- August 29 (The Beheading of John the Baptist)

Prohibited Seasons:
- The Advent Season, November 15–December 23
- Great Lent, including Cheesefare Week and Bright Week
- The Fast and Feast of the Dormition of the Theotokos (August 1–15)

In an emergency case (such as a military leave or the illness of a parent) when a wedding needs to take place during a prohibited time, a dispensation must be received from the metropolitan or hierarch.

Once you have a tentative date in mind, contact your priest to see if he and the church are available on that date. Do not make plans or order invitations until you have met with the priest. Once you have finalized the date with your priest, discuss with him whether there are any fees for the wedding and/or the rental of the hall for the reception.

MARRIAGE PREPARATION COUNSELING

Marriage preparation counseling is necessary to help support a successful marriage. Your priest will inform you of the number of premarital counseling sessions he wants to have with you before the wedding. During these sessions, the religious, social, physical, emotional, and moral issues of marriage will be discussed. It is important to learn what marriage means to Orthodox Christians.

WHO MAY MARRY?

For an Orthodox priest to be allowed to celebrate a marriage, at least one of the two spouses must be of the Orthodox Faith. The non-Orthodox spouse must have been baptized in a Christian church in the Name of the Holy Trinity. A marriage between an Orthodox Christian and a non-Christian or an individual not baptized in the Name of the Father, Son, and Holy Spirit cannot be celebrated in the Orthodox Church.

SPIRITUAL PREPARATION

If you are an Orthodox Christian, you are urged to receive the Sacrament of Confession and the Sacrament of Holy Communion as preparation for your marriage. By so doing you will bring a new vitality, spirit, and bond to your marriage that will enhance and deepen your lives together.

If you are not an Orthodox Christian, you are urged to partake in some form of spiritual preparation guided by your parish priest/pastor that will prepare you spiritually for your marriage. I also urge you and your fiancé(e) to attend together any Introduction to the Orthodox Faith classes your parish may offer. These classes will give you an appreciation for and an understanding of your fiancé's faith. If you desire to embrace the Orthodox Faith, you must first be properly instructed over a period of time. At the very least, the priest may suggest that you read certain introductory books on the Orthodox Faith.

Of course, no one is ever coerced to accept the Faith. Marriage in the Orthodox Church does not mean membership in the Orthodox Church for a Christian who is not Orthodox.

PAPERS, DOCUMENTS, AND CERTIFICATES

The Orthodox Christian getting married must be a member in good standing of an Orthodox parish. If either of you belongs to an Orthodox parish other than the one where the wedding will take place, you must obtain a letter from your parish priest attesting to your spiritual standing and membership. You will also need a copy of your Baptismal Certificate.

If you are not Orthodox, you must obtain a copy of your Baptismal Certificate that will verify you were baptized in the name of the Holy Trinity. If the non-Orthodox partner has not been baptized, or has not been baptized in the name of the Holy Trinity, the parish priest will discuss the issue with you in detail.

If you were born outside the United States and came to this country after your eighteenth birthday, a certificate verifying that you are single and eligible to marry should be obtained from your home country parish priest, signed by the bishop of the home country diocese.

Previous Civil Divorce

If either of you has been divorced, you must give a certified copy of the entire divorce decree to the priest. If an Orthodox partner had a previous marriage blessed in the Orthodox Church, the original ecclesiastical divorce decree must be given to the priest.

It is also necessary to petition the archbishop and the ecclesiastical court for your restoration to the sacramental life of the Church, since divorce breaks that communion. Such a petition is drawn up by you and the priest and should include the date and reason for the divorce, reconciliation attempts, and your desire to come back into communion with the Church. All such petitions are considered on an individual basis and are, of course, confidential.

A Marriage License

A marriage license issued by the county wherein the wedding will be held must be in the possession of the priest before the marriage service can take place. The license to get married is valid for thirty days.

CONCERNING THE WEDDING CEREMONY

The Sponsors and the Wedding Party

The best man and maid/matron of honor must be practicing members of the Orthodox Faith and members in good standing of an Orthodox parish. The other members of the wedding party do not have to be members of the Orthodox Faith, but they must be Christians and must agree to observe the practice of the Orthodox marriage ceremony. The size of the wedding party should be discussed with the priest.

Dress Code
Common sense, guided by the norms of Christian modesty and the decorum befitting a church ceremony, should be used in selecting the gowns for the bride and bridesmaids. Please remember that the bridal headdress should not prevent the placing of the wedding crown during the service.

Rings and Crowns
Every marriage in the Orthodox Church is solemnized with two rings and two crowns. Discuss with the priest whether the church will provide the crowns, or whether you must provide your own.

Music
Only the traditional music of the Orthodox Church may be used during the marriage ceremony. You may request to have either the church choir or a chanter be present at the service. Any outside vocalist, as well as the music to be sung, must be approved by the priest.

   Musical instruments are generally not used during the marriage ceremony. Check with your priest to see whether instruments are acceptable before or after the ceremony. In some parishes, an organ may be played prior to the wedding and for the processional and recessional.

Flowers and Decorations
Orthodox churches are beautiful and colorful with or without flowers. Since space is limited, visibility and access for movement during the ceremony must be taken into account. If flower arrangements are used, discuss their size and number with your priest.

Photographs
Your photographer must speak with the priest prior to the service to understand what is and what is not permissible before, during, and after the service.

Visiting Clergy

Any invitation to another Orthodox priest or bishop to concelebrate the wedding ceremony is extended by the local priest. The participation of non-Orthodox clergy is generally limited to remarks at the end of the service. This must be discussed with the local priest, and the invitation to non-Orthodox clergy is extended by the local priest.

Length of the Ceremony

The Orthodox marriage ceremony is approximately 45 minutes, depending on the length of the processional and recessional. It is good to plan for about one hour from beginning to end. Again, non-Orthodox elements may not be added to or incorporated in the Orthodox Sacrament of Marriage.

IN CONCLUSION

Because marriage is a Sacrament of the Church, you are expected to be a practicing Orthodox Christian, striving to live the Faith and participating in the Divine Liturgy on a regular basis. It is essential that you receive the Sacraments of Confession and Communion before the wedding, as a proper preparation for this great event. Make time before your wedding to be prayerful, asking for God's blessing, strength, and help as you embark on your long journey together. May God grant you many years!

THE ORTHODOX WEDDING CEREMONY

At last, the hour of your wedding is at hand! This, for you and yours, is a day like no other. For your understanding and edification, what follows is an overview of the wedding ceremony itself, beginning with the betrothal.

THE BETROTHAL

The Questions
When the groom and the bride with their sponsors stand before the Holy Table, the priest begins by asking the groom, "Have you, N., a good, free, and unconstrained will and a firm intention to take unto yourself to wife this woman, N., whom you see before you?" In a loud voice the groom replies, "I have." The priest asks the bride the same question.

This question was introduced by the Church in order to protect both partners from being forced into a marriage against their will. In the ancient world, and in tribal societies, force and fear were sometimes exercised regarding marriage. In the event one of the parties responds, "No, I have not," the Church protects and shelters that person from harm.

The Candles
Once both have answered, "I have," each is presented with a lighted candle. This signifies that the couple's journey begins with the light of Christ. His light will illumine their lives and their marriage.

129

Christ said, "You are the light of the world . . . Let your light so shine before men, that they may see your good works and glorify your Father in heaven" (Matt 5:14–16). Let your light shine in your marriage in front of your spouse. Each of you is given a candle. Both the husband and the wife have their own candle, their own walk with God. Throughout marriage, we never put our candles out. When we bring our candles together, the amount of light is doubled.

I have been present at non-Orthodox weddings where the bride and groom each have a candle, and together they light a third candle. Then they both blow out their individual candles. The third candle is called a "unity candle," symbolizing that two lives are becoming one.

We Orthodox certainly acknowledge that the two become one, but we do not understand marriage as the extinguishing of our individual personalities. Marriage is the place for the lights of both husband and wife to shine even more brightly together. Both spouses bring the light of Christ with them into their marriage, and the amount of light in the home increases.

In one of his parables, Christ told of ten people waiting for the arrival of a wedding party. Five of those waiting showed wisdom because they brought sufficient oil to keep their lamps burning until the arrival of the wedding party. The other five foolishly brought no extra oil with them. Their lamps went out, and while they went to buy more oil, the wedding party arrived and went into the wedding feast, and the doors were shut. When the foolish ones returned, they were told it was too late and were turned away at the door (Matt. 25:1–13).

The parable has many applications and levels of meaning. However, the last verse of the parable tells us plainly, "Watch therefore, for you know neither the day nor the hour" (Matt 25:13).

The message of the candles is clear. Guard the light of Christ in your life and in your marriage. Guard the light of your love for each other. Do not let the cares of this world, of business and of busy schedules and even of children, cause you to neglect either your relationship with Christ or your relationship with each other.

You are overflowing with love for each other now. Your happiness knows no bounds. But be careful lest you foolishly think the love and happiness of your wedding day is enough to carry you through a long life together. Remember, most tires do not go flat from a blowout, but from a slow leak.

The Supplications

A litany is offered for the couple whom God has brought together. Whom God has brought into unity, let no one put asunder. God ordains an indissoluble bond of love that will make this couple, like Isaac and Rebecca, heirs of His promise.

This new life for the couple begins in the house of God, not in a back yard or a country club. The church is the safe haven, pure and undefiled, born as a virgin among the Gentiles, protecting us from a sinful world. Likewise, the couple is born anew out of this sinful world, born anew with a pure beginning. Thus, we ask God to "send down upon them perfect and peaceful love."

We should be reminded that the Church is perfect as the Body of Christ, but it has a human face. The congregation is always "under construction" as it makes its way on the journey of being made into the likeness of God. So, too, your marriage is a work in progress. Each couple must constantly labor to deepen their love for each other. In the betrothal, we have prayed for you. But prayer is not restricted to the church. Pray for yourselves and for each other throughout your married life.

The Rings

The betrothal service began with the question of whether the groom with a free and unconstrained will has a firm intention to take this woman for his wife. The same question was asked of the bride. Their verbal agreement, "I have," is now translated into a commitment by means of rings placed on the couple's fingers. Rings are tangible and visible. They announce, proclaim, and identify the wearer as committed and pledged to love the other forever.

First, the priest takes the bride's ring and blesses the groom with it three times. He then places the bride's ring on the groom's finger. Next, the priest takes the groom's ring and blesses the bride with it three times. He then places the groom's ring on the bride's finger.

Each has been blessed by the very ring they are giving to the other. They are saying to each other, "You are a blessing to me." The groom and bride now exchange rings, and each wears the one intended for him or her.

THE MARRIAGE SERVICE

The Holy Table
The betrothal having been completed, the marriage service begins at the holy table placed in front of the iconostasis. Upon the table are candles, the Gospel book, a cross, the common cup, and two crowns.

The priest takes up the censer and begins censing each side of the table, the bridal couple, and all those present. As he censes, he (or the choir) sings Psalm 127 (LXX). This psalm is also read in the Jewish wedding ceremony. It is a road map for couples in the Word of God.

    ⇛ *Blessed are all they that fear the Lord and walk in His ways.*
    At the outset of your journey as a married couple, you are told you will be blessed if you guard your relationship with God and walk in the path He sets before you. Then the Psalmist tells you exactly how you will be blessed.

    ⇛ *Thou shalt eat the fruit of thy labors: O blessed art thou, and happy shalt thou be.*
    You are not promised a silver spoon and a life of luxury. You are called to a life of working together to build a home and a life. Marriage is work that bears fruit. Those who work at their marriages will eat the fruit produced by their common work. You will be blessed with happiness.

    Many couples confess the happiest time in their lives was when they were just starting out together—having very little and struggling to make ends meet. Those couples who continue to serve God and continue to labor together in their marriage will continue to reap a harvest of joy through the years.

    ⇛ *Thy wife shall be as a fruitful vine upon the walls of thy house, thy children like a newly-planted olive orchard round about thy table.*

Our rationalized Western world is filled with schedules and regulations. Before we know it, the world around us intrudes with its demands and squeezes the vitality out of us and our marriage. So we must be on guard. Women are the source of life; they alone can give life. In a home and marriage that honors God, the wife will flourish. She will bring art and beauty to the walls of the house and to the life of the home.

Your home will be filled with love and life, and out of that life children will be born. A marriage filled with love, in which the wife is blessed to flourish, will create a home your children will return to through the years. Not only while they are little, but even more when they are grown and married, will they return and gather joyfully around the family table.

There are many strange voices in our world telling young couples their careers are more important than a fruitful home filled with children. They promise a life of self-indulgence and little responsibility. They offer a vision of child-free adulthood. God, on the other hand, offers the blessing of life, vitality, fruitfulness, and genuine happiness for those who walk in His ways. His ways most often include children.

↬ *Lo, thus shall the man be blessed that feareth the Lord. The Lord in Zion shall so bless thee, that thou shalt see the good things of Jerusalem all the days of thy life.*

God will bless you when you walk with Him. The groom, who will become a husband and father, must take on the responsibility to work, to provide, to support the physical, psychological, sociological, and financial needs of his family. The bride, who will become a wife and mother, will work side-by-side with her husband in creating a home filled with life and love. She may even need to work outside the home for a season as she helps her husband provide for the family.

But in all the work and struggle to make ends meet, to provide for children, to pay for braces and then college, the couple must never lose sight of God. A couple who continues to honor God as the source of their lives and their home will delight in the things of God and the services of His Church. The Church is the New Jerusalem, the holy city, the dwelling place of God upon the earth. A couple whose marriage is grounded in worshipping regularly and in supporting their church financially will be blessed. They will delight to "see the good things of Jerusalem" all the days of their lives.

∾ *Yea, thou shalt see thy children's children, and peace upon Israel.*
Young couples getting married are not thinking about grandchildren. But they themselves are grandchildren. At many weddings the grandparents are present as honored members of the family. We do not exist in isolation from our heritage or the generations before us, whose DNA we carry within us.

Grandchildren are a joy and a blessing. They mark the continuity of our lives. And it is in the Church that the joy of grandchildren is lived out fully. Your marriage begins in the Church. Your home will be sustained by the Church. Your children will be baptized and raised in the Church.

But the real blessing comes when you see your children's children being baptized in the Church you have loved and that has shaped your life. By God's grace, the day will come when you witness your children's children standing in front of this same holy table with a priest singing Psalm 127 over them.

Someday your time on earth will end. It will be this Church that stands with your children and grandchildren as we together usher you into heaven. It will be your children and grandchildren who will offer a forty-day memorial service for you and commemorate you with each passing year, singing, "May your memory be eternal." And you will rest in peace where the just repose.

The Kingdom of God
Weddings in the ancient Church were celebrated during the Divine Liturgy, as were the other sacraments. Over time, the marriage service became a separate sacramental service.

The Divine Liturgy begins with the priest proclaiming, "Blessed is the

Kingdom of the Father, and of the Son, and of the Holy Spirit: now and ever and unto ages of ages." So as the next step in the marriage service, the priest stands before the holy table. With the Gospel book he makes the sign of the cross and chants the same proclamation.

The Christian life is lived in the Kingdom of God. This Kingdom is not restricted to the church building. It is not only in our worship, but in the living of our lives that the Kingdom of God is made present.

The wedding ceremony may be distinct from the Divine Liturgy, but it is still taking place within the Kingdom of God. Your marriage is a sacrament of the Kingdom and is to be lived through transformation by the Kingdom. Christ Himself told us, "Seek first the Kingdom of God and His righteousness" (Matt. 6:33), and everything else will be added to our lives.

The prayer that follows the proclamation of the Kingdom is patterned after the Great Ektenia of the Divine Liturgy. It is a prayer offered for peace and the salvation of all who are present—who in turn are praying for the well-being of the bridal couple by singing, "Lord, have mercy." We pray not only for your marriage, but that your marriage will bring continual salvation to you both, and also to us.

Models to Emulate
We live in a world that makes it very easy to get a divorce. So many marriages have failed that some today do not believe a successful marriage is even possible anymore. In despair, people opt out of marriage and choose instead to simply live together.

But in Christ, you have chosen to believe a successful marriage is possible. The Church holds that a successful marriage is achievable, and that permanence ought to be the norm for Christians. But the Church is not naïve. She knows successful marriages become so through the grace of God and hard work.

The best examples of successful marriages may be found in the Bible. These are men and women just like us whom God brought together. In spite of the challenges they faced, these couples were committed to God and to each other, and God blessed them.

The priest now offers a special prayer of blessing for you, naming specific examples of successful marriages from the Scriptures. Here is a small portion of that prayer:

Bless them, O Lord our God, as You blessed Abraham and Sarah.

Bless them, O Lord our God, as You blessed Isaac and Rebecca.

Bless them, O Lord our God, as You blessed Joachim and Anna.

Bless them, O Lord our God, as You blessed Zacharias and Elizabeth.

Abraham and Sarah left Mesopotamia at God's command and traveled to Egypt before settling in Palestine. Rebecca left her home and traveled to Palestine to marry Isaac, a man she had never met. Joachim and Anna, in their old age, became the parents of the Virgin Mary, the Mother of our Savior. Zacharias and Elizabeth, also in old age, gave birth to John the Baptizer, the Forerunner of Christ. We ask God to bless you, the bridal couple, in the same way He blessed all of these couples.

By the grace of God in their lives, these marriages survived the challenges of life. God blessed them and preserved them through the storms of life even as he preserved Noah and his family in the ark. God protected them during the fierce fires of trials and conflict even as he protected Shadrach, Meshach, and Abednego (Daniel 3:1–97, LXX).

We pray for gladness to come upon you, but not just a generic gladness. We pray for the same gladness experienced by Helena when she discovered the precious Cross upon which Christ was crucified. It is only in the Cross that we find salvation. It is only in the Cross that marriages are filled with gladness and joy, which in turn preserves and protects your love, your relationship, and your marriage.

Finally, in this prayer we give thanks for your parents, who have nurtured you and whose prayers have formed a firm foundation within you. We give thanks for your friends who stand with you as witnesses.

Now that you are a couple, you are encouraged to find older couples who have worked out their marriage in spite of trials and difficulties. Find other young couples who are beginning their married life and who are committed to their marriage and the Church. Surround yourself with good models of husbands and wives working on having a successful marriage.

The Sacrament of Creation

The prayer for your marriage to be blessed is followed by another prayer. This is a very sacred and holy moment. We are taken back to the Garden of Eden, where God created man out of the dust, fashioned his wife from his rib, and joined her to him as his helpmate, his partner and companion for life.

Here we call upon God to join the two of you together, just as He joined Adam and Eve, for only by God can a man and a woman be truly united in one mind and one flesh. We are asking that you be united not only socially, culturally, and spiritually, but sexually. God has made us male and female that we might find love, companionship, and sexual joy in the arms of our wife or husband. And out of this warm and loving sexual relationship, we ask God to grant you children, children that you will raise in the knowledge and love of Him.

As you start out in married life, your home is fresh and new, bright and pure. It is your own Garden of Eden, full of promise and hope. In this garden your children may play and learn and grow to be faithful adults and fellow servants of God.

But you must remember there was a snake in the first garden. Snakes will seek entrance into your garden too. By the grace of God and an active spiritual life in the Church, the snakes can be defeated. But you must always be watchful. Never take your marriage and your Garden of Eden for granted.

The Crowning

The high point of the second part of the service is the crowning, when crowns are placed on the heads of the bride and groom. These crowns have two primary meanings: they are crowns both of martyrdom and of royalty.

On the one hand, the crowns represent the crown of thorns that was placed on the head of Jesus. An Orthodox marriage is a marriage in Christ. A couple with Christian values living their married lives in commitment to Christ will be subject to ridicule in today's world. A couple who believe they must guard and protect their love, who turn to the Church for guidance and wisdom in building their marriage, may be subject to mockery. A couple who take seriously their pledge of being faithful to each other will be out of step in today's culture.

The Church reminds us of the concrete reality of a Christian marriage. Marriages are constantly under attack. The enemy will whisper in your ears, urging you to abandon your vows and reject your commitment to each other. The crowns are there to remind you that you will endure difficult times, times when it will be easy to listen to the evil whisperers. But the crowns also remind you that by faithfulness, perseverance, and obedience to Christ, your marriage will succeed and bring forth joy. St. Paul wrote at the end of his life, "I have fought the good fight, I have finished the race, I have kept the faith. Finally, there is laid up for me the crown of righteousness" (2 Tim. 4:7–8).

In the Orthodox Church, crowns are associated with martyrdom. The word *martyr* means "witness." In a Christian marriage, the husband and wife bear witness to the presence of Christ in their lives by having a home that is centered in Him.

Martyrdom also refers to the relationship between husband and wife. For the marriage to become an "us," each must yield to the other. Both must be willing to die to self in order to become one flesh with each other. In a Christian marriage, being a martyr does not mean being henpecked or browbeaten. A Christian marriage involves a mutual martyrdom whereby both husband and wife die to themselves in order to live together in Christ.

Finally, the crowns are symbolic of royalty. Christ not only wore a crown of thorns, but He is now crowned King of kings and Lord of lords. Likewise, the groom and bride are crowned as king and queen of their home. Your home is your kingdom—regardless of whether it is a mansion or a small apartment. As king and queen, you now have the responsibility to provide for your kingdom and protect it from external threat and internal turmoil. You must rule your kingdom with fairness and compassion for all those in it, or your kingdom will suffer and your marriage may be lost.

In the ceremony, you are crowned each to the other. Mutual crowning speaks of mutual equality within the marriage. The husband is not the wife; neither is the wife the husband. There is no subordination. The husband and wife are an equal team united in a common oneness, a common unity in the living and sharing of life itself.

The Epistle

The epistle reading comes from Ephesians 5:22–33. In this passage, St. Paul instructs the couple regarding their attitude towards each other. To the bride, he says, "submit yourself to your husband." The word "submit" means "to voluntarily place oneself under"—much as a priest would do with his bishop. Both are equal in Christ, but there is order in the relationship.

St. Paul then compares the relationship of husband and wife to that of Christ and the Church. He insists, not once but three separate times, "Husbands, love your wives as Christ loved the Church." Christ died for the Church. We are talking here about servant leadership. A husband is to love his wife as he does his own body. A husband must see that his love is manifested in both a spiritual and physical relationship. Marriage without love, honor, and respect will not long exist. A wife desires—no, a wife requires—love, honor, and respect if she is to reciprocate with honor and submit to her husband.

The Gospel

The Gospel reading is John 2:1–11, the story of the wedding at Cana. It is here that the first of Christ's miracles occurred. His presence indicates His approval and blessing of marriage and His involvement in the everyday affairs of life.

Jesus and His Mother attended a great wedding feast. This was a Middle Eastern Jewish wedding that lasted for many days. The master of the feast had supplied six stone water pots filled with twenty or thirty gallons of wine each. By the third day they were running out of wine. Mary, learning this, told Jesus, "They have no wine."

Water sustains life. But it is wine that gives joy to life. Mary does not beg, whine, or complain. She simply tells Jesus, "They have no wine." You must be careful not to run out of wine, or joy, in your marriage. The wine of a joyful marriage cannot be bought; it comes from a prayerful life. Mary, the Mother of our God, is your intercessor. She interceded for this couple, and she will intercede for you. Just ask her.

The six stone jars normally held water. Now that they were empty, Jesus had the servants fill them with water again, and He turned the water into wine. Christ turns little apartments into kingdoms of joy. He transforms small acts and simple gifts into extravagant experiences of joy and happiness. Christ transforms life.

When the master of the feast tasted the new wine, he said to the bridegroom that most people serve their best wine first, and then, if they need more, they serve a lesser wine. But in this instance, he said, "You have kept the good wine until now!"

Your wedding is a day of great joy. Your pictures will show a bride and groom beaming at each other. This is the first wine, and it is good. But the best wine awaits you in the years ahead—twenty-five, thirty, fifty years down the road. Don't ever settle for water. Christ still turns water into wine.

The Lord's Prayer

In the marriage ceremony we pray the Lord's Prayer, taken from the Sermon on the Mount (Matt 6:9–13). Our Lord taught us how to worship and how to pray. The Lord's Prayer is also the disciples' prayer. It is the prayer of all who follow Christ.

In the Orthodox practice, the priest always says the liturgical ending to the Lord's Prayer: "For Thine is the Kingdom, and the power, and the glory of the Father, and of the Son, and of the Holy Spirit, now and ever and unto ages of ages." To which all those present add, "Amen." This reminds us that in the Incarnation of Jesus Christ, our God has revealed Himself as Trinity. He is Father, Son, and Holy Spirit, undivided, of one essence, one God. Even as God is Trinity—a single unity—so too the union of husband and wife, though they are two people, is a single unity.

Although the Lord's Prayer is often prayed privately, flowing out of our personal relationship with God, it also is recited corporately by the Church. We are participants in a larger picture than just ourselves. Our marriages are established publicly, within the larger realm of family and church. Though separate and singular, no marriage is lived in isolation from family and friends.

In the Lord's Prayer we pray, "Give us this day our daily bread." As husband and wife you may now pray this prayer together. St. Paul told the Christians in Thessalonika, "If anyone will not work, neither let him eat" (2 Thess. 3:10). To succeed, a marriage takes work—work on the relationship, the work of creating and maintaining the home, and work outside the home for economic stability.

The two of you are now in this together. You have a common Father who loves you and who will provide for you the sustenance of life as you include Him in your home. You share a common Savior—the Son, the Bread of Life—who gives life to each of you as you approach the chalice. The Holy Spirit now abides in your marriage and in your home to lead you and to guide you in the paths of righteousness that will bring you abundant life. He will deliver you from evil as He guards you from being led into anything that could harm your marriage.

Make the Lord's Prayer your own. Say it together, out loud. Say it daily—at a meal together or before going to sleep. Praying this prayer together will strengthen your marriage by helping you acknowledge God as Lord of your marriage and your home. In this prayer you pray together for God's Kingdom, His power, His glory, His provision, and His protection to come into your home and marriage.

The Common Cup

As we mentioned before, in the early Church the Sacrament of Holy Matrimony took place during the Divine Liturgy, as did all the other sacraments. In the Divine Liturgy the Holy Eucharist is consecrated and distributed to the faithful. In the wedding service, the Eucharist is symbolized by the common cup of sweet wine.

Only the groom and the bride are invited to partake of this cup. Your marriage is private and intimate. You have freely chosen each other and forsaken all others.

Each of you is given three sips from the cup. The priest sings, "I will take up the cup of salvation, and call upon the name of the Lord." This verse, Psalm 115:4 (LXX),[16] is a eucharistic verse, for it refers to "the cup of salvation," which is the chalice. But it is also the song of your marriage. In your marriage you will find the way of salvation and call upon the name of the Lord together.

Your common cup is filled with sweet wine. As you share your life together, through joy and sadness, you will discover how sweet the wine of life can be.

The Dance of Isaiah

In just a few minutes your marriage ceremony will be concluded. It will not be long before you go to your reception. As you enter the room, the wedding party will burst forth in joyful celebration and exuberant dancing.

Likewise now, in the marriage ceremony, we approach a pinnacle as you have

∞   entered the church
∞   said, "I have"

---

16 Psalm 115:4 (LXX) is found in a Protestant Bible as Psalm 116:13.

- ∞ held the candle of Christ's light
- ∞ exchanged the rings
- ∞ stood before God and smelled the incense
- ∞ been blessed by God as He blessed Abraham and Sarah
- ∞ joined your hands together
- ∞ received your crowns
- ∞ heard St. Paul's message to love one another
- ∞ heard the wedding Gospel of Cana
- ∞ offered your prayer to your Father in heaven
- ∞ received the sweet wine from the common cup.

Just as we will do at the reception to follow, it is time for us to dance and celebrate liturgically. The groomsman holds the right hand of the groom, the groom holds his bride's right hand with his left, the bride holds her bridesmaid's right hand with her left, and together they follow the priest as they "dance" or process three times around the holy table. The priest leads them with the cross, censing as they go.

The priest sings, "O Isaiah, dance for joy! For a Virgin was with child and hath borne a son, Immanuel, both God and man, and Orient is His name: whom magnifying we call the Virgin Blessed."

Seven hundred years before Christ, the prophet Isaiah foretold the coming of Christ when he said, "Therefore the Lord Himself will give you a sign: Behold, the virgin shall conceive and bear a Son, and shall call His name Immanuel" (Isaiah 7:14). "For unto us a Child is born, unto us a Son is given" (Isaiah 9:6).

Isaiah waited seven long centuries before his joy could explode in dancing and celebration at the fulfillment of God's promise. He had seen the coming of the Lord, born of a Virgin, giving Himself for our salvation. And now that it has come to pass, O Isaiah, it is time to dance.

Likewise for you, groom and bride, what you have planned for, what you have envisioned happening, is now here. Your union has been publicly acknowledged and blessed by God before the congregation. It is time to dance! We celebrate your love, your marriage, and your future together. We celebrate the possibility of children, new life, and the embracing of the future.

I remember when our son Philip was born. I went to the hospital to visit

Sharon and to look in on Philip. I remember standing in front of the window at the maternity ward waiting for them to bring our son to the window.

Next to me another man stood, also looking through the window at the babies. He was bowing his head towards each baby. After he finished, I asked him, "Is that part of your tradition?"

"No," he said. "I just wanted to bow to honor each baby. I don't know what they might become—maybe doctors, lawyers, scientists, teachers, businessmen, the president, maybe a prophet or prophetess."

Then he said, "God bless them, and God bless their mothers."

I asked, "How about their fathers?"

He grinned and said, "God has already blessed them."

Your parents are blessed this day. Your family shares in your joy. They have looked forward to this day longer than you have. And like Isaiah, who waited seven hundred years, they too are ready to dance and celebrate the coming of this moment.

The second time around the holy table, the song to the holy martyrs will be sung. "Ye holy martyrs, who fought the good fight and have received your crowns, entreat ye the Lord that He will have mercy on our souls."

We have already spoken of the crown of the martyrs. Your joy at finally beginning your married life together is tempered by asking the holy martyrs to intercede for you. Marriage is martyrdom. We must die to being single, to acting and thinking as a single person. We must die to this world for the sake of our partner in this life. Both of you are laying aside your private and single lives in order to take up together the life of being a couple, joined in Christ.

St. Paul tells us, "But you, O man of God, flee these things and pursue righteousness, godliness, faith, love, patience, gentleness. Fight the good fight of faith, lay hold on eternal life, to which you were also called and have confessed the good confession in the presence of many witnesses. I urge you in the sight of God . . . that you keep *this* commandment without spot, blameless until our Lord Jesus Christ's appearing" (1 Tim. 6:11–14).

If St. Paul were at your wedding, he might put it this way: "Flee from those things that put your relationship and your marriage at risk. Instead do those things that are right and good, that increase your faithfulness and love for each other. Especially learn to be gentle with each other. Be kind and forgiving. Your marriage is worth fighting for. Take hold of the life you have chosen together, the life you have confessed before God and us here assembled together. Keep your vows without stain and without shame. Look forward to the future of your marriage with as much joy and anticipation as you have on this day, at the beginning of your marriage. And our great God and Savior Jesus Christ will bless you all the days of your life, even unto His appearing."

Those who work at, protect, defend, and honor their marriage will grow to love each other in ways you as newlyweds cannot imagine. In due time, such a couple's invisible crowns will almost become visible to those watching you as a couple.

Finally, we begin our third dance as we go around the holy table once more. This time we sing, "Glory to Thee, O Christ our God, the Apostles' boast, the martyrs' joy, whose preaching was the consubstantial Trinity."

We give glory to God on behalf of you, the couple. You have accepted the proclamation of the Son as your Savior Jesus Christ, and have the Holy Spirit dwelling in your lives. You have chosen a Christian wedding so that your marriage may be an example of faith and trust in God. The Apostles proclaimed the faith, they suffered martyrdom, but they did not compromise the faith. They fought the good fight, they finished the course, and they received the crown of righteousness.

We pray the same for you—that you will fight for your marriage, that you will be kept spotless, blameless, and without reproach, unto ages of ages. Amen.

Removal of the Crowns
You have literally been crowned king and queen of your own home and marriage. The physical crowns you wore during the marriage ceremony represent the invisible crowns you now wear. The priest will remove the physical crowns. No one but you can ever remove your invisible crowns. It is the prayer of the Church that the day never comes when you decide to abdicate your throne, abandon your marriage, and remove your crown.

The priest now prays the prayers of exaltation for each of you. He prays for the bridegroom to be exalted like Abraham and blessed like Isaac, and to multiply like Jacob and have a large family. He prays for the bride to be exalted like Sarah, exult like Rebecca, and multiply like Rachel.

These men, the ancient patriarchs of Israel—Abraham, Isaac, and Jacob—and their wives, Sarah, Rebecca, and Rachel, remind us that we are not identical. Abraham, Isaac, and Jacob were three very different men and husbands. Sarah, Rebecca, and Rachel were three very different women and wives. God blessed each of their marriages, but their marriages were not identical.

Your marriage will be unique. It will not be identical to either of your parents' marriages, or to the marriages of your friends. We exalt you, bless you, and multiply the fruitfulness of this *your* marriage. Learn from Abraham and Sarah, Isaac and Rebecca, and Jacob and Rachel. Ask God to add to your life and marriage what was good and strong from each of their marriages, from your parents' marriages, and from the marriages of others. Add all this to what is already good and strong in you.

Before the crowning, the priest asked God to "unite them." Now that the physical crowns are removed, the priest asks God to bless those who "are now united together in wedlock." Somehow, while you were wearing your crowns, holding your candles, praying and dancing, the mystery of marriage occurred. The sacrament of being joined together, united together, happened. The physical crowns can be removed. The invisible crowns now remain.

Prayers are now offered for the protection and preservation of your marriage. We ask that God will receive your crowns into His Kingdom in order that your crowns—and your marriage—will be preserved spotless, blameless, and without reproach. It is by your choices that each of you will remain pure in your marriage.

A lady once remarked, "I used to pray for newlyweds to have a happy life. Now I pray they stay married." Sadly, not all marriages survive spotless, blameless, and without reproach. Make no mistake. There are no cheap divorces. The breakup of a marriage comes with a huge emotional and financial price tag. You cannot stand at the Holy Table with your fingers crossed, thinking to yourself, "If this doesn't work, I can always get a divorce." Marriage is not a game. This is for keeps.

The Nuptial Blessing and Dismissal Prayer
The marriage ceremony concludes by asking God to bless you, giving you a long life together, healthy children, earthly good things, and a life of faith with the promise of the life to come.

The dismissal prayer reminds you that many are praying for you and your marriage. The Theotokos, the Mother of God and our great intercessor, is praying for you. The Apostles are praying that a life of faith will be deeply rooted in your marriage. Saints Constantine and Helen are praying that you will defend the kingdom of your marriage. And the Great Martyr Procopius, who embraced martyrdom with the same enthusiasm as a bridegroom embraces his bride in marriage, prays that you will take hold of your marriage crowns with the same determination with which he claimed the crown of martyrdom.

Surrounded by family and friends, with the prayers of the saints, the priest blesses you with the cross. The Amen is sung.

CONGRATULATIONS!

It is done. The wedding is over. Your months of meticulous planning and preparation are over. The reception awaits you. Then you are off to begin your life together. There will be the joyful coming together in the consummating of your marriage. There will be that first home to create. There will be so many things to discover about each other—physically, emotionally, and spiritually. There is so much you do not yet know about life and each other. You are like Adam and Eve when everything is brand new and waiting to be discovered.

Embrace the paradise before you. Look to the future with faith and hope and love. Pray for a fruitful womb, that your home will be filled with the noise and excitement of children. Embrace life to the fullest. With the light of Christ to guide you, with your faith nurtured by the Church, and with the prayers of the saints and all who love you, as the king and queen of your own marriage, take each other's hands. Your kingdom awaits. In the Name of the Father, the Son, and the Holy Spirit, One God. Amen.

Epilogue

THREE PEARLS OF WISDOM
CONCERNING MARRIAGE

ST. JOHN CHRYSOSTOM

Known along with Basil the Great and Gregory the Theologian as one of the Three Holy Hierarchs, St. John Chrysostom is considered the greatest preacher in Christian history. He lived in the late fourth century.

> Do you want your wife to be obedient to you as the Church is to Christ? Then take upon yourself the same providential care of her that Christ takes upon Himself for the Church. And even if it becomes necessary for you to give your life for her, yes, and even to endure and undergo suffering of any kind, do not refuse it. Even though you undergo all this, you will not, not even then, have done anything equal to what Christ has done. For you indeed are doing it for someone to whom you are already joined, but He did it for one who turned her back on Him and hated Him. . . . Through affection, through kindness you will be able to lay her at your feet. For there is no influence more powerful than these bonds, and especially for husbands and wives.[17]

---

17 St. John Chrysostom, cited by John Meyendorff, *Marriage: An Orthodox Perspective* (Crestwood, NY: St. Vladimir's Seminary Press, 1984), 70–71.

TERTULLIAN

Known as the father of the Latin Church, Tertullian wrote the following to his wife in the early third century AD.

> How shall we ever be able adequately to describe the happiness of that marriage which the Church arranges, the sacrifice strengthens, upon which the blessing sets a seal, at which angels are present as witnesses, and to which the Father gives His consent.
>
> How beautiful, then, the marriage of two Christians, two who are in one hope, one desire, one in the way of life they follow, one in the religion they practice.
>
> They are . . . both servants of the same Master. Nothing divides them, either in flesh or in spirit. They are, in very truth, two in one flesh; and where there is but one flesh there is also but one spirit. They pray together, they worship together, they fast together; instructing one another, encouraging one another, strengthening one another.
>
> Side by side they visit God's church and partake of God's Banquet; side by side they face difficulties and persecution, share their consolations. They have no secrets from one another; they never shun each other's company; they never bring sorrow to each other's hearts. Unembarrassed they visit the sick and assist the needy. They give alms without anxiety; they attend the Sacrifice without difficulty; they perform their daily exercises of piety without hindrance.
>
> They need not be furtive about making the Sign of the Cross, nor timorous in greeting the brethren, nor silent in asking a blessing of God. Psalms and hymns they sing to one another, striving to see which one of them will chant more beautifully the praises of their Lord.
>
> Hearing and seeing this, Christ rejoices. To such as these He gives His peace. Where there are two together, there also He is present; and where He is, there evil is not.[18]

18 Tertullian, in a letter to his wife, ca. 202. Retrieved from www.crossroadinitiative. com on 12/09/2010.

A PROFESSOR COMMENTS ON ST. PAUL

The main theme of St. Paul is that the husband and wife form a unity or whole. They are distinct from one another and are not so just by virtue of their marriage, but also by their very nature. In this, the apostle is only repeating the doctrine of Genesis, and on the strength of it, he concludes that the husband's love for his wife is natural and necessary.

To love one's wife means simply to love oneself, i.e. one who is not only similar but identical with oneself. The wife is something more than an image of her husband, she is a part of him, a whole with him. But in spite of this equality their relationship may not be reversed. Just as Christ does not depend on the Church but the Church on Christ, so also the wife becomes a wife because of her husband.[19]

---

19 Professor Serge Khoskoy, cited by Constance Tarasar, *Woman: Handmaid of the Lord*, 127.

ABOUT THE AUTHOR

Fr. Constantine Nasr has served for thirty-seven years in the pastoral ministry of the Antiochian Orthodox Christian Church. He has counseled starry-eyed couples about to be wed, and he has stood in the trenches with those fighting to save their marriages. He has rejoiced with those celebrating their fiftieth wedding anniversaries, and he has wept with those whose marriages failed. He has conducted Marriage Encounter Seminars across the country. Married for thirty-eight years and the father of two,  he understands firsthand the pressures on a marriage and a family. Honestly and frankly he confronts those issues that must be mastered for marriages to succeed.